MAHĀYĀNA BUDDHISM IN ĀNDHRADEŚA

By

Dr. J. Sitaramamma

Eastern Book Linkers

DELHI : : (INDIA)

Published by
EASTERN BOOK LINKERS
5825, New Chandrawal,
Jawahar Nagar, Delhi-7
Ph. : 23850287, 30919869
e-mail : ebl@vsnl.net

First Edition : 2005

Price : 300.00

ISBN : 81-7854-064-9

Mahāyān Buddhism in Andhradeśa by Dr. J. Sitaramamma

Type Setting by Creative Graphics, Delhi
Printed at : R.K. Offset Process, Delhi-32

DEDICATED TO

My Beloved Teacher

LATE PROFESSOR B.S.L. HANUMANTHA RAO

with

gratitude and affection

ACKNOWLEDGEMENTS

I am very much grateful to my late Professor B.S.L. Hanumantha Rao for his deep affection and scholarly guidance without which the present work would not have been successfully completed by me. His valuable advice and guidance enabled me in completing this work in time for which I am beholden to him.

I am highly thankful to Dr. S. Nagaraju, formerly the Professor of History in the University of Hyderabad for his guidance in the preliminary stages of my work. I am highly indebted to Prof. N.H. Samtani for his timely help, and writing a foreword to this book.

My thanks are due to the Librarians and the staff of the Nagarjuna University Library, French Institute of Indology Library, Pondicherry and the Osmania University Library, Hyderabad.

I will be failing in my duty if I do not thank the Eastern Book Linkers, for having printed in the book form. My special thanks are due to Prof. K.C. Suri for his valuable suggestions.

I record my gratitude to my colleagues and the non-teaching staff of the Centre for Mahayana Buddhist studies with whose encouragement I could complete my work according to schedule.

J. SITARAMAMMA
Centre for Mahayana Buddhist Studies
Nagarjuna University (A.P.).

PREFACE

Buddhism had been a strong force in the social and cultural history of Āndhradeśa for about 1000 years. The new gospel was responsible for uniting the Āndhras into a single race and in return the Āndhras played a remarkable role not only in its geographical extension but also in developing and enriching the Buddhist philosophy and religion. The Āndhras appear to have been in the forefront of all the movements that took place in the development of Buddhist doctrine.

In the evolution of Buddhism the three phases viz. Hīnayāna, Mahāyāna and Vajrayāna or Tantrayāna are recognised as the most important. The Āndhra Buddhists being realistic, reacted to the socio-economic and religious situation in the land and tried to reform their system from time to time to make it more agreeable to people but at the same time basing the reforms on the deeper teachings of the Buddha. The discussions they carried on in their Vihāras led to the rise of Mahāyāna which gradually led to the emergence of Vajrayāna. Further the social, economic and religious conditions at the time of the advent of Buddhism in Āndhradeśa proved very congenial for the new developments.

Different scholars have propounded different theories regarding the Original Home of Mahāyāna. But a careful study of the literary and archaeological sources reveal that

Āndhradeśa was the birth place not only of the Mahāyāna system but also of many philosophers that developed it.

Several scholars and archaeologists in the days of the East India company brought to light innumerable Buddhist sites. The most important of them are Robert Sewell, Cunningham, Alexander Rea, James Joice Burgess, Longhurst and following their lead Indian archaeologists like R.Subrahamanyam and T.N.Ramachandran who brought to light innumerable Buddhist sites, spread over the length and breadth of Āndhradeśa. In the course of these excavations quite a good number of inscriptions were (also) unearthed. But most of these archaeologists cared more for the architectural features of the Buddhist monuments and the artistic beauty like that of Amarāvati and Nāgārjuna-koṇḍa sculptures. They paid very little attention to the development of Buddhism as a philosophical and religious system during the period.

In recent years an attempt is being made to bring out in clear terms the rise and growth of different phases of Buddhism namely Theravāda, Mahāyāna and Vajrayāna and highlight the part played by the Āndhra Buddhists in their development and spread. Dr. M.Rama Rao wrote a small book entitled *Buddhism in Āndhradeśa.* But it is not at all comprehensive. N.Ramesan in his *Glimpses of Buddhism* touched upon the role of the Āndhras in the history of Buddhism. As it is a quick survey of Buddhism in general, much attention could not be focussed on the contribution of Āndhras in particular.

P.S. Sastri in his articles published in The Indian Historical Quarterly wrote about the Buddhist philosophers who lived in Āndhradeśa. As his views and conclusions, are without much reference to the available archaeological materials, they are not altogether dependable.

B.S.L. Hanumantha Rao in his book entitled *Religion in Āndhra,* devoted a chapter to Buddhism in Āndhradeśa and tried to outline the part played by the Andhakas and their sub-sects in the development of the principles and practices which led to the rise of Mahāyāna and ultimately Vajrayāna. However it also being a general survey his work also is not as comprehensive as one expects.

K.Satchidananda Murty has discussed the contribution of Āndhras to Buddhist Thought in general and highlighted the part played by Ācārya Nāgārjuna in shaping the Mahāyāna system in his small book entitled *Nāgārjuna.*

The present study is an attempt to give a comprehensive and connected account of the rise and growth of Mahāyāna in Āndhradeśa making use of the original literary sources such as *Prajñā Pāramitā, Gaṇḍavyūha* and *Ratnāvalī,* the accounts of foreigners like Yuan Chwang and Tārānātha and the archaeological epigraphical and sculptural materials so far unearthed and brought to light. The published modern works on the subject are also referred to.

An effort is made in this study to establish that Āndhradeśa is the original Home of Mahāyāna Buddhism. Short biographical sketches of the philosophers who were responsible for the systematisation of Mahāyāna and for the later developments in it, such as Acarya Nāgārjuna and Āryadēva, Bhāvaviveka Buddhapālita, Diġnāga and Dharmakīrti are also added. The impact of Mahāyāna on the Āndhra's socio-economic and cultural life has been briefly outlined, basing mainly upon the evidence of inscriptions.

I am aware of my limitation of knowledge of this vast subject , although its borders are limited, hence I feel I may have left some important aspects. I hope the subject will further be studied in all its dimensions which will be helpful in the region wise study of Mahāyāna Buddhism in India. I would seek indulgence of readers for any lapses and omissions in the present work.

J. Sitaramamma
Centre for Mahāyāna
Buddhist studies
Nagarjuna University (A.P.)

August 2001

FOREWORD

I am glad that Dr. J. Sitaramamma's much awaited work *Mahāyāna Buddhism in Āndhradeśa* is finally published. I must congratulate her for this important publication, which in my view covers many aspects of the development of Buddhism in Andhra. In fact it is the first of its kind in its exhaustive treatment of the subject, I also pay my compliments to the Eastern Book Linkers, Delhi, who have published this notable work.

In four chapters, Dr. Sitaramamma has covered the origin of Mahāyāna Buddhism and its development in ancient Andhra Pradesh. The work is extensively annotated which reflects the perseverance of the scholar. She has shown how Āndhradeśa has been the original home of Mahāyāna, although it gradually spread throughout India and even crossed the borders of the country.

The author has also thrown a good light on biographical sketch of the Mahāyāna philosophers of Āndhradeśa who systematized the Mahāyāna doctrines. Dr. Sitaramamma's view that controversies which were raised by the Andhaka sects were instrumental in the rise of Mahāyāna cannot be disputed as we find these significant controversies in abundance in the early Pali canonical text of the *Abhidhamma Pitaka, viz. Kathāvatthu* (Trans. : *The Points of Controversy)*. The textual evidence on the history of schools indicates that these Andhaka sects were related to the Mahāsaṅghika schools, the precursors of the full-fledged developed Mahāyāna school.

The author also rightly observes that the great Mahāyāna philosophers like Nāgārjuna, Dignāga and Dharmakirti lived in Āndhradeśa. In fact, Āndhradeśa was the great centre of literary and religious activity, especially in the development of Buddhism. Some of the important pilgrimage centres like Amarāvatī and Nāgārjunakoṇḍa are also found in present Andhra Pradesha. She has also mentioned their importance from the religious, cultural and architectural aspects.

The book has a good bibliography and index. I hope the present work will be well received by the scholars as well as the lay readers.

Sugata Kutir **N.H. Samtani**
Varanasi-221010
6 April 2004

ABBREVIATIONS

A.I.	:	Ancient India.
I.A.	:	Indian Antiquary.
I.H.Q.	:	Indian Historical Quarterly.
J.R.A.S.	:	Journal of Royal Asiatic Society.
J.A.S.B.	:	Journal of Asiatic Society of Bengal.
B.S.A.J.	:	Buddhist Stūpas of Amarāvati and Jaggayyapeṭa.
E.I.	:	Epigraphica Indica.
L.L.	:	Luders List.
M.A.S.I.	:	Memoirs of Archaeological Survey of India.
A.R.A.S.	:	Annual Report of Archaeological Survey of India.
E.R.E.	:	Encyclopaedia of Religion and Ethics.

CONTENTS

Acknowledgements (v)

Preface (vii)

Foreword (xi)

Abbreviations (xiii)

Chapter I

Introductory, Mahāyāna, Origin, Meaning and Features : 1-23

Origin of the word Mahāyāna - Mahāyāna, its meaning and use - Hīnayāna versus Mahāyāna-Features of Mahāyāna Buddhism.

Chapter II

Original Home of Mahāyāna Buddhism : 24-64

North-Western Origin-Orissa Theory-Thoery of Āndhra Origin, Date of Āndhra Buddhism-Condition of Āndhra during the time-Social, Economic and Religious Conditions-Epigraphical Evidence and Literary Evidence.

Chapter III

Mahāyāna Philosophers of Āndhradeśa : 65-99

Ācārya Nāgārjuna-Āryadēva-Buddhapālita-Bhāvaviveka-Dignāga and Dharmakīrti.

Chapter IV

Impact of Mahāyāna on Life and Society : **100-121**

Society: Condition of the Women, Selfless Social Consciousness-Impact on Economy-Literary activity-Development of Philosophy and Logic-Centres of Learning, Art, Religion. Resume

Bibliography 122-130

Index 131-140

CHAPTER - I

INTRODUCTORY

Mahāyāna, Origin, Meaning and Features

The emergence of Mahāyāna during the early centuries in or before or after the Christian era is considered as a veritable revolution[1] in the thought and practice of Buddhism. With its rise, both the aims of Buddhist religious practice and the means of achieving those aims underwent a radical change.

Mahāyānism was no doubt a break away religion. But it was not altogether a new religion. Its roots are to be traced to the very life and teachings of the Buddha. Immediately after the *sambodhi,* for several weeks the Buddha thought to keep his knowledge for himself, as the common people could not understand and practice it[2]. But after some contemplation, and as the legend goes, with the intervention of Sahampati Brahmā, he decided to share his enlightenment with the suffering mankind[3]. It is in this deep concern of the Buddha for the mankind and his desire to save them by removing their ignorance (avidyā), which is the root of sorrow and suffering, one can see the beginnings of Mahāyānism. After this resolve the Buddha started on his missionary career.[4]

The Buddha was teacher of extraordinary patience and capacity. He devised his teachings to suit the intellectual levels and mental capacities of each whom he taught. According to the *Saṁyuttanikāya,* [5] Buddha has classified people into different grades according to their mental capacities, as land is graded according to its fertility. According to him, people are of three different categories—excellent, mediocre and dull and taught in such a way that each one of them could understand and practise his teachings. To the common people his teachings were only a code of morals intended for self-improvement and for promoting harmonious social life. They were satisfied with them. Such teachings are known as Vyakta upadeśa or exoteric teachings which constitute the original or the basic teachings of the Buddha.[6] To the highly intellectual persons who could understand deeper things, he taught very intricate subjects subtle issues of philosophy. The people with their higher intellectual qualities could go deep into the ontological perception of the Buddha and develop his teachings. These are guhya upadeśa or the esoteric teachings, [7] which were expounded and elaborated through the writtings and commentaries of great luminaries like Acarya Nāgārjuna, Āryadēva, Dignāga, Bhāvaviveka, Asaṅga, and Dharmakirti over a long period of time. The result was the rise and development of Mahāyāna.[8]

Therefore Mahāyāna was only a developed form of Buddhism, having its roots in the very teachings of the Buddha. Edward Conze rightly remarks : "Buddhism throughout its history has the unity of an organism, in that, each development has taken place in continuity from the previous one. There is in Buddhism no innovation, but what seems so is in fact an adaptation of pre-existing ideas".[9]

Nor the emergence of Mahāyāna system was sudden. It developed doctrine by doctrine through centuries taking into its fold not only the doctrinal developments but also the changing situations in the religious and socio-economic conditions in the land. Further it is not "a single vehicle but rather a train comprising many carriages of different classes."[10] As Buddhism expanded geographically it had to reconcile with the local cults, adopting some of their principles and practices, as a result of which the original code of discipline had to be enlarged and modified.[11] In addition, as Sir Charles Eliot says that changes were bound to take place in the original teachings of the Buddha because: (1) he did not leave behind any written word and naturally doubts and disputes arose regarding the interpretation and even the very text of his teachings and (2) he did not prescribe any rites regarding birth and death and allowed his lay disciples to follow their earlier practices.

Further by about the second century B.C. there were remarkable changes in the religious life in the land. By that time, Buddhism made rapid progress because of the patronage it received from the great monarch Aśoka Maurya.[12] From being a local cult Buddhism developed into a national or an international religion.[13] Alarmed at the popularity of Buddhism, Brahmanism reconciled or popularised with Bhāgavatism in order to check the growth and popularity of Buddhism.[14] Brāhmanism became less ritualistic and more devotional and attracted even foreigners like the Indo-Bactrians and Schythians into its fold.[15] The neo-Brāhmanical system posed a serious threat to Buddhism. After Aśoka's death, Buddhism lost royal patronage.[16] The successors of Mauryas, the Śungas in the north and the Sātavāhanas in the south were stout champions of Brāhmanism with leanings towards Bhāgavatism.[17] Buddhism had to depend more and more upon the patronage of the rich Śreṣṭhi and Gahapati classes.[18] Thus Buddhism had to face several challenges from the orthodox system with its emphasis on self-centered asceticism (attainment of their own enlightenment) was not equal to meet them.

Therefore Āchāryas like Nāgārjuna and Āryadēva with a practical eye on the realities and needs of the situation tried to reform Buddhism and the result was the development of Mahāyanism.[19] The Japanese scholar Daisaku Ikeda has therefore rightly said "certain unusually keen and enlightened members of the monastic community, dissatisfied with the attitude and practices of Hīnayāna Buddhism, joined forces with the more spirited and imaginative leaders among the laity in a co-operative venture to carry out reforms and the result was Mahāyānism".[20]

ORIGIN OF THE WORD MAHĀYĀNA

It is very difficult to trace the origin of the words Mahāyāna and Hīnayāna. In the Second *Saṁgiti* held at Vaiśāli the Saṅgha was split up into the Theravāda and Mahāsāṅghika schools.[21] Some scholars think that the schism took place on the issue of *Daśa vatthūni,* [22] the ten (novel) practices adopted by the Vajjian monks. But according to others the split was caused by the famous five points of Mahādeva.[23] The ten practies were purely disciplinary whereas the five points of Mahādeva were doctrinal.

In the Second Council, after a long discussion the Vajjian practices were rejected as opposed to the *Vinaya* by the President, Sabbakāmi.[24] Those who supported the president came to be known as the Sthaviravādins or Theravādins.[25] Those who supported the Vajjian monks were expelled from the Saṅgha.[26] The latter summoned their own Council which was attended by 10.000 monks.[27] Because of the large number comprising of their saṅgha, they called themselves as Mahāsāṅghikas.[28] As the Mahāsāṅghikas tried to introduce new practices in the discipline, not sanctioned by the Vinaya and tried to propagate them, they were taken by the Theravādins to be opposed to the Dhamma. Therefore they called the Mahāsāṅghikas as Adhammikas (Adhārmikas) and Pāpabhikkhus[29] (sinful monks), etc. These descriptions naturally pained and angered the Mahāsāṅghikas who wanted to retaliate and to establish the superiority of their own system. They too started calling the Theravādins by names.

In the early Buddhist literature we come across words like Ēkayāna and Dviyāna, Bodhisattvayāna and Śrāvakayāna and Buddhayāna and Arhatayāna.[30] The first systems in these three groups were held superior to the second ones. Ēkayāna means unique *yāna* whereas *Dviyāna* means only secondary yāna. Bodhisattvayāna is always superior to Śrāvakayāna and the aim of Buddhahood is naturally much higher than Arhathood. Therefore Dviyāna, Śrāvakayāna and Arhatayāna were used by the Mahāsāṅghikas to denote the Theravāda in order to castigate it as an inferior system.[31] The Mahāsāṅghikas were still unsatisfied with these terms and desired to use a more pungent term to describe their rivals. Finally they coined the words Mahāyāna and Hīnayāna. Mahāyāna (great vehicle) Hīnayāna is the old original inferior system.[32] These words gradually gained currency.

MAHĀYĀNA - ITS MEANING AND USE

Mahāyāna in the words of Sir Charles Eliot was "indeed a great movement which in its various phases may be regarded as a philosophical school, a sect and a church."[33] It is an unselfish quest for enlightenment with the noble aim of the emancipation of the entire mankind. That is why the *Prajñāpāramitā* says that "The Mahāyāna is as big as the sky that could accommodate all the human and divine beings and carry them to nirvāṇa."[34] This meaning has been amply brought out by scholars who have used the word from time to time.

Scholars are keen in finding two distinct phases in the use of the word Mahāyāna. These are: (1) The Sūtra period and (2) the school period. The Mahāyāna Sūtras are generally known as the *Vaipulya sūtras*. They are: *Prajñāpāramitā, Avataṁśaka, Saddharma Puṇḍarīka, Gaṇḍavyūha, Suvarṇaprabhāsa, Tathagataguhyaka, Ratnakūṭa, Laṅkāvatāra sūtra, Amitāyurdhyāna, Dasabhūmikā Sūtra, Vimalakīrti Nirdeśa, Sukhāvatīvyūha, Samādhi Rājasutra,* etc. They cannot be attributed to any single author. They were the outcome of a collective efforts discussions and deliberations of a group of monks concentrated on disclosing and unfolding their own doctrines. They formulated the Sūtras on which ultimately Mahāyāna came to be based. During this period in the use of the word Mahāyāna there is no indication of criticising and rejecting the doctrines of others as inferior. But gradually there appears to have developed a keen rivalry between the two schools. Therefore one has to prove the inferiority of the other doctrine, reject it and try to establish the superiority of one's own system. The words then were used to indicate an ontological division, striking out at the same time a comparison of one school with the other.

AŚVAGHOSA:–The first great Buddhist writer to use the word Mahāyāna was Aśvaghoṣa who is believed to have lived at the court of the emperor Kanishka (A.D. 124-148).[35] There is of course a controversy about Kanishka's date. Many scholars prefer to place him between A.D.78 and 102.[36] Some ascribe to him the date A.D. 124-148. Aśvaghoṣa is regarded more a poet than a philosopher. He was indeed a poet-philosopher. In his works, the word Mahāyāna occurs four times, but it was used not to denote a separate system of religion and philosophy. It was used only in the sense of the law of perfect Buddha. However, in the writings of Aśvaghoṣa, especially in his *Buddhacarita*, there are clear indications of transition from Hīnayāna to Mahāyāna.[37] In this work Aśvaghoṣa explains the theory of anātman and said that this is the Mahāyana, the instrument of the law of the perfect Buddha.[37-a]

NĀGĀRJUNA

It is universally agreed that Acārya Nāgārjuna has systematised and propagated Mahāyāna Buddhism. In his commentaries on *Prajñā-Pāramitā*, Ācārya Nāgārjuna says that Śrāvakayāna: was for the individual salvation, whereas the Mahāyāna was for the benefit of the entire mankind.[38] Philosophically, Mahāyāna stands on a higher plane than Hīnayāna. Nāgārjuna says in the same work that Śrāvakayāna believed in the śūnyatā of the individual entity (pudgalaśūnyatā) but Buddhayāna asserts the śūnyata not only of individual entity but even of cosmic existence (sarvaṁ śūnyam).[39] In the Avataṁśaka sūtra, quoted by Kimura, Nāgārjuna says, "All people in the Mahāyāna can accomplish 'sarvajñānamārga' without any hindrance and all people can arrive at the realm of bliss by that sarva jñānayāna"[40] The Ratnāvalī of Nāgārjuna describes Mahāyāna as possessing every merit and absolute good alone is dear to it, because it does not take into consideration what is good for oneself. Whoever hates it is damned.[41] In the same work he asks : "Karuṇā pūrvakaḥ sarve niṣyaṁdajñāna nirmalāh uktāyatra mahāyāna kastam niṁdeṭ sacetanaḥ." How could a man in full possession of mental faculties abuse the great vehicle where it is stated that all results are preceded by compassion purified by wisdom

At another place he says:

Guṇadoṣā nabhijñova doṣa samjni guṇeṣuvā athāvāpi guṇadveṣī mahāyānasya niṁdakaḥ.

A man abusing the great vehicle is one who does not distinguish between merits and sins or one who takes merits to be defects or one who hates merits.[43]

Regarding Mahāyāna finally Nāgārjuna says, it is the soul of all sentient beings (*sarva-sattva*), it constitutes all things in the world, phenomenal and super-phenomenal and through this soul we can disclose what the Mahāyāna signifies".[44]

Āryadēva, the disciple and successor of Nāgārjuna compares Hīnayāna and Mahāyāna. He tries to prove the worthlessness of the former and extols the superiority of the latter. At one place he says, "The people of the small vehicle (Hīnayāna) are afraid of death at every step; their achievement of victory in war lies indeed very far off; while the men of the great vehicle (Mahāyāna) are clad with the armour of mercy; they are intent on saving the world and are fully equipped with the bow and arrows of sympathy and morality.[45]

In his *Prajñā Pradīpa,* a commentary on the *Mādhyamika Śāstra,* Bhāvaviveka says that Saddharma (true law) is pure and it can do away with all sorts of sufferings as well as their semblances. Therefore it is described as pure and hence Mahāyāna.[46]

While the above philosophers established the greatness of Mahāyāna, Asanga strongly criticised Hīnayāna and declared the superiority of Mahāyāna. He says that in all the five aspects of religious belief and practice Mahāyāna is superior to Hīnayāna:in aspiration, in teaching, in the way of livelihood and in the period of exertion. In all these aspects Hīnayāna is very narrow, while Mahāyāna is Noble and higher. The Hīnayāna aspires for individual salvation which it thinks possible in three births and the monopoly only of ascetic way of life. On the other hand, Mahāyāna aspires for the acquisition of merit as well as wisdom, which was possible even for virtuous upāsaka and with which he strives indefinitely till the entire mankind is saved.[47] Vasubandhu, the brother of Asanga in his *Saddharma Puṇḍarīka Sūtra Śāstra* compares Hīnayāna to Milk and Mahāyāna to Cream.[48] According to all these philosophers, the Buddha preached that all beings possessed the nature of Buddha. But Hīnayānists who do not believe in it will not be able to attain (nirvāṇa)[49] Buddhattva or Buddha hood.

HĪNAYĀNA VERSUS MAHĀYĀNA

As already noted, both Mahāyāna and Hīnayāna are rooted in the teachings of the Buddha. Therefore both schools have deep faith in the *Buddhavacana*. These two schools accepted the fundamental principles of Buddhism embodied in the First Sermon. Both of them believed in *Anatta, Anicca* and *Dukkha,* the theory of *Paṭicca-samuppāda* or dependent origination. It begins with four noble truths (*ārya satyāni : dukkha, Samudaya, Nirodha* and *Mārga*). Everything is transitory (anicca) and with out any self (anatta)—belief in the non-ego. The world has no end.[50] Delusion is the cause of suffering which is universal.[51] Moral practices mentioned in the eightfold noble path and the Pāramitās are prescribed in order to remove delusion.

But Hīnayāna looks upon Buddha only as a Tathāgata a historical person who aims at reforming the contemporary religious system. No doubt, the Theravādins or Hīnayānists have the concept of Bodhisattva, but for them Śākyamuni is Bodhisattva only before the attainment of Buddhahood. They are opposed to the introduction of even the slight deviation in the original canon and believed in the efficacy of ascetic life for the attainment of the arhathood, which is their aim.[52] Because of its rigid orthodoxy it came to be known as Kaṭhinayāna.[53] They paid no attention to the popular religious sentiments and requirements. Hence inspite of the eminence of the Hīnayāna writers and the magnificence of richly endowed Hīnayānic monasteries, the older form of Buddhism began to lose its hold upon the people and give way to a new movement.

The new movement was Mahāyāna which tried to rectify the drawbacks of the old system. In the words of the Japanese scholar Chizen Akanuma "The Mahāyāna movement is a movement of the revival of Śākyamuni's teaching which was about to die out as a result of the realistic teaching of Hīnayāna".[54]

FEATURES OF MAHĀYĀNA BUDDHISM

As already noted the principles of Mahāyāna are to be traced to the original canon. In the words of Sir Charles Eliot, "Their ideas of Mahāyāna are all to be found in the Nikāyas, some times as mere seeds, some times as well-grown plants".[55] However the new system has developed and in the Mahāyāna there are certain features which distinguish it from the Hīnayāna. They are as follows:

1. Divinity of Buddha
2. Trikāya Theory
3. Bodhisattva Doctrine
4. Devotionalism
5. Altruistic Morality
6. Eligibility for Laity
7. *Dharma Sūnyatā*
8. Ideal of Buddhahood.

DIVINITY OF BUDDHA

The Mahāyāṇa conceived the Buddha as supernatural. He is transcendental, eternal and absolute. The Mahāyānists believe that the Buddha by his transcendental wisdom sees all things from their inception to their final disappearance. His eye surveys everything to its destiny. In the Saddharma puṇḍarīka, Gautama Buddha is described as the loving father of all creatures and all pious Buddhists are exhorted to worship and adore him.[56] The *Sukhāvatī-vyuha* promises rebirth in the Amitābha Buddha's paradise (Buddhakṣhetra) to all those who think of him and utter his name with love and devotion.[57] According to the Saddharma Puṇḍarīka Buddha is not an ordinary deity, but the Devātideva, the paramount god. He is the creator of all Bodhisattvas. Whoever practises the pāramitās, engages in devotional observances become Buddha. The one thing needful is faith (Śraddhā).[58]

As a consequence of this conception a cosmic function has been attributed to the Buddha. As Lord Supreme, Ādi Buddha, he would be sending into the world

Buddhas and Bodhisattvas whenever necessity arises to save the suffereing mankind. From his skandhas emanated the five Dhyāni Buddhas:[59] Amitābha, Akṣhobhya, Vairocana, Ratnasambhava and Amoghasiddhi. Thus there developed the theory of innumerable Buddhas.[60] Gradually a huge pantheon has been developed with innumerable gods and goddesses attending upon the Ādi-Buddha.

TRIKĀYA THEORY

The supernatural conception of Buddha led to many other theories. In it was rooted the Mahāsānghika belief that Buddha was Upapāduka or self born.[61] This belief in its turn developed into the Trikāya theory. According to it, Buddha is conceived as the essence of all beings (Dharmakāya).[62] The Buddha has a glorious divine form Sambhogakāya.[63] He assumes at will various forms (Nirmāṇakāya) to deliver beings from delusion to propagate the Dharma.[64] These three appearances are meant one for men and one for gods and one for the highest beings, respectively. The Trikāya theory is the heart of the Mahāyāna. When a Buddha assumed the Nirmāṇakāya in order to establish contact with the world in a human form, it is assumed that it is for the time being for a specific purpose. The Rūpakāya the actual physical body of the Buddha is visible to every one whereas the Nirmāṇakāya is visible only to adepts. When a Buddhist takes refuge in the Buddha it is in the eternal Dharmakāya.[65]

3. BODHISATTVA

The most striking feature of Mahāyāna is the growth of the concept of Bodhisattva. The word Bodhisattva is very old and occurs even in the Pāli *Nikāyas*.[66] Buddha also speaks about himself as a Bodhisattva before he attained *Saṁbodhi*. The concept receives full development in the *Mahāvastu*[67] and *Lalitavistara*.[68]

The word Bodhisattva means an enlightened being.[69] In Tibetan, Bodhisattva is translated as a being with "Heroic mind".[70] Sir Charles Eliot says."Bodhisattva means one whose essence is knowledge."[71] L.D.Barnett calls him a "Creature of enlightenment".[72] D.T.Suzuki describes him as an "intellectual being".[73] A careful study of Bodhisattva reveals that he possesses all the above qualities.

In the early Mahāyāna the Bodhisattva occupies a position next to the Buddha. He has all the qualifications to become a Buddha. Later Bodhisattva is regarded as equal to the Buddha in many respects. In *Saddharma-Puṇḍarīka* it is stated that Avalokiteśwara advises Kāśyapa in the following manner: Just as one worships the new and not the full moon, just so those who believe in me should know the Bodhisattvas, and not the Tathāgatas or "From the Buddha arise only the disciples and Pratyeka Buddhas" - but from the Bodhisattva the perfect Buddha himself is born.[74] Love, compassion, mercy, grace, pity are the important qualities of Bodhisattva. According to Mahāyāna Buddhism any one who develops Bodhicitta is a Bodhisattva i.e. a being destined to attain Bodhi (enlightenment) and becomes a Buddha in the long run. In fact every Mahāyānist is a Bodhisattva aiming at Buddhahood. Though the Buddhahood is within his easy reach, Bodhisattva takes the vow that he would postpone his attainment and help the entire world to Nirvāṇa. The hero of Vimalakīrti nirdeśasūtra, Vimalakīrti says that "As all other beings are sick, so I am sick, All beings are considered as one".[75] A Bodhisattva helps the entire world to Nirvāṇa, practising Pāramitās over countless births.

Pāramitā means the highest acquisition of a particular virtue. The word *Pāramitā* has been translated as transcendental virtue', perfect virtue', 'highest perfection'.[76] The six *Pāramitās* are really the chief factors in Bodhisattva's discipline. Later four more *Pāramitās* were added but they are supplementary in character. They are:

1. *Dāna* (Liberality)
2. *Śīla* (morality or righteousness)
3. *Kṣānti* (forbearance)
4. *Vīrya* (energy)
5. *Dhyāna* (rapt musing)
6. *Prajñā* (wisdom)

The four supplementary pāramitās are:

1. *Upāya-Kauśalya* (skilfulness in expediants)
2. *Praṇidhāna* (vow or resolution)
3. *Bala* (strength or power)
4. *Jñāna* (knowledge)

A Bodhisattva is required to acquire all the ten virtues perfections in order to qualify himself for the attainment of Buddhahood. Of those the most important is *Upāya, Kauśalya* D.T. Suzuki gave the meaning of *Upāya-Kauśalya* as expedient strategem', 'device' or 'craft', It has a technical sense in Buddhism.[77] It is used in contrast to intelligence or knowledge *(Prajñā)*. So, Vimalakīrti says in the Sūtra bearing his name (chap. 8, verses 1-4): *"Prajñā is the mother of the Bodhisattva and skilful Upāya is his father; there is no leader of humanity who is not born of them"*.[78]

The doctrine of *Pāramitā* was evolved and by way of illustration, story after story was composed resulting in the accumulation of huge Jātaka and Avadāna literature. Further the Bodhisattva has to pass through the ten stages of spiritual development,[79] and *Daśabhūmisūtra* is the standard treatise on the subject.[80] A Bodhisattva especially cultivates one of the Pāramitās in each of the bhūmis.

The Bhūmis are as follows:-

1. *Pramuditā* (joyful)
2. *Vimalā* (pure)
3. *Prabhākarī* (Brilliant)
4. *Arciṣmati* (Radiant)
5. *Sudurjayā* ("Very difficult to conquer, ")
6. *Abhimukhī* (to see face to face)
7. *Dūraṅgamā* (Far-going)
8. *Acalā* (Immovable)
9. *Sādhumati* (good mind)
10. *Dharmameghā* (Cloud of the Law)

Among the Bodhisattvas who ranked almost as gods were: 1. Avalokiteśvara, 2. Mañjuśrī, 3. Maitreya, and 4. Vajrapāṇi. Among these, Avalokiteśvara is the personification of compassion, whereas Mañjuśrī is the personification of wisdom.[81]

4. DEVOTION AND WORSHIP

The natural accompaniment of the deification of Buddha and Bodhisattva is devotion to them. The Mahāyānist *bhakti* is laden with *mantras* and *dhāranīs.*[82]

The Mahāyānist takes the vow that rites efface sin and attributes salutary virtue to the reading of *sūtras* and the repetition of the name of the Buddhas.[83] In the Mahāparinibbāna Sutta, there are directions for erecting

Stūpas and Caityas.[84] After the rise of the Mahāyāna, images of Buddha were installed at cardinal points of the Stūpas and Caityas were built with images. They were worshipped with flowers, lamps and garlands.[85] An elaborate ritualism of worship (*pūja*) was evolved.

Even the Bodhisattvas should observe religious practices, perform worship, etc. with devotion and faith. The *Ratnameghasūtra* describes the method of worship and it recommends the chanting of hymns in praise of Buddhas and Bodhisattvas.[86] The worship by illumination is also prescribed in Śikṣāsamuccaya.[87] It is by that feeling of fervent devotion combined with the preaching of active compassion that the creed has enlisted the sympathy of millions of people and has become a factor of much greater importance than the orthodox Buddhism in the history of mankind.[88] The devotees covered India with temples and Caityas filled with images in the belief that merit accrued both to donors and to the artists.

5. ALTRUISTIC MORALITY

The keynote of Mahāyāna ethics was extreme altruism. The ideal of Bodhisattva and the practice of six Pāramitās clearly bring out this aspect. It is in short the realisation of non-dualism.[89] According to the Mahāyānists the effacement of self could only be achieved in course of several lives, through the service of others. A Mahāyānist must take the vow that he would not seek his own happiness, heavenly life, even Nirvāṇa unless and until he is able to do his bit to make all other beings happily attain heavenly life and ultimately realise nirvāṇa. Buddha is described as having been imbued with the idea of the happiness and welfare of the entire mankind *Sarva, Sattanu Kampassa lokahita.*[90] In Amarakośa, Buddha is called as an *advayavādi*.[91] As a corrolary the Mahāyāna lays emphasis on great compassion' *Mahākaruṇā* which characterises the Bodhisattva. It is always the aim of Bodhisattva: "In all lands may all the sufferings of living beings come to an end... May those who suffer hunger and thirst receive food and drink in abundance... May the blind see, deaf hear, the pregnant women give birth to a child painlessly ..." Bodhisattva think, "It is indeed better that I alone suffer than all living beings should reach the abodes of the evil forms of existence." In Mahāyāna the compassion *(Karuṇa)* is rooted in knowledge *(Prajñā)* which concept may be traced back to the fundamental teachig of the Buddha about anatta (non-ego). If there is no ego then there is no difference between one ego and another. In the excercise of compassion therefore the truth of there being no distinction between the I and Thou *(Parātmasamatā)* and is known through feelings".[92] Consistent with such realisation, the Mahāyānists developed the concept of transfer of merit. The Mahāyānist makes gifts with the prayer that the merit which accrues from it should make all people happy and finally then attain nirvāṇa. The Bodhisattva proclaims" all merits which I have acquired here without concern give up for the welfare of all beings".[93]

In Mahāyāna the sublimest religious ideal, that of absolute altruism, it conjoined with the realisation of the profoundest metaphysical truth, that of anatta or no-self. The Bodhisattva of the Mahāyāna represents not the mere juxtaposition but the living spiritual unity of these two basic themes of Buddhism.[94]

THE PLACE OF LAITY

The Bodhisattva ideal of Mahāyāna makes no

difference between Bhikkhu and Upāsaka. According to it the family life is no hindrance to practise spiritual values and hence the rigid monasticism was given up. The *Vimalakīrtinirdeśasūtra* clearly establishes this point. The principal character in the Sūtra, Vimalakīrti impresses that house-hold life was not a hindrance to achieve enlightenment and Bodhisattvahood. Vimalakīrti is shown to have possessed knowledge, superior even to that of Bodhisattvas like Mañjuśrī.[95]

Being a rich merchant, he could not only understand the true nature of things but also realising *parātmasamatā.* Thus "With passage of time old inhibition receded into the back-ground, " moreover the theory of "perfection in expedient means *upāya-kauśalya pāramitā* naturally required and encouraged proficiency in various arts and sciences."[96] As a result, the literature and art of the Mahāyānists were produced not only by monks and nuns but also by *upāsakās* and *upāsikās.*

ŚŪNYATĀ

The realisation of *Śūnyatā* is fundamental to Mahāyānism. Buddhism teaches *anatta (anātma).* The Hīnayānists deny the existence of *ātma* and they believe in *pudgala-śūnyatā*. The Mahāyānists go a step further, they deny even the existence of the objective world and believe in *Dharmaśūnyatā*. But *Śūnyatā* does not imply that all is negation. It means that all things are mere manifestations. The Supreme reality in this world, is the law of change. Therefore Śūnyatā does not mean absolute non-being but relative being. According to the *Mañjuśrī-mūlakalpa,* Ācarya Nāgārjuna refuted the view that every thing exists as well as the view that every thing does not exist. For the Mahāyānists śūnyatā is therefore the absolute reality. It can be realised only when both kleśāvaraṇa (the veil of defilement) and Jñeyāvaraṇa (the veil of ignorance) are removed.[97]

IDEAL OF BUDDHAHOOD

For the Mahāyānist, Arhahood is not ideal. A Mahayanist believes that every one is a potential Buddha. By practising the Aṣṭāngamārga and by preaching the Brāhma viharas, realising enlightenment Sarvam-Śūnyam and advayam one can attain the highest stage of Buddhahood.[98] This new point of view led to the identification of the Buddha with the truth, the reality.

REFERENCES

1. T.R.V.Murti, *Central Philosophy of Buddhism*, (London, 1980), pp. 5-6.
2. F.Max Muller (ed.), *Vinaya Texts*, Vol. 13, Part-1, *Mahāvagga*, Sacred Books of the East (Delhi, 1982), pp. 84-85.
3. *Ibid*, p. 86.
4. N. Dutt, *Early Monastic Buddhism* (Calcutta, 1980), pp. 93- 94.
5. Edward Conze (ed.), *Buddhist Texts Through the Ages*, (New York, 1954), p. 34.
6. Ryukan Kimura, *A Historical Study of the Terms Hīnayāna and Mahayana and the Origins of Mahāyāna Buddhism*, (Delhi, 19), pp. 16-18
7. *Ibid*.
8. *Ibid*, pp. 159-189.
9. Edward Conze, *Thirty Years of Buddhist Studies,* (London, 1967), p. 75.
10. Sir Charles Eliot, *Hinduism and Buddhism,* Vol.I, (London, 1971), pp. 4-5.
11. G.C.Pande, Studies in the origin of *Buddhism*, (Delhi, 1974), pp. 558-59.
12. R.K. Mukherji, Aśoka, (London, 1972), pp. 260-261.
13. B.S.L.Hanumantha Rao, *Religion in Āndhra,* (Guntur, 1973), p. 55.

14. Grierson, "Bhakti Mārga", *Encyclopaedia of Religion and Ethics*, Vol. II, pp. 539-551.
15. R.C. Majumdar and Pusalkar (Ed.), *The Age of Imperial Unity*, (Bombay, 1968), p. 98. The Śunga period saw the revival of the Brāhmanical influence and the growing importance of Bhāgavata religion. which made even the Greeks among its votaries. Heliodorous became a Vaiṣṇavite. Among the Sakas there were kings like Rudradāman - Rudradamanikā.
16. The Buddhist tradition is not complementary to Puṣhyamitra and describes him as a cruel persecutor of Buddhism. He is said to have destroyed monasteries and killed monks in course of his march to Sakala, where he declared a prize of one hundred gold coins on the head of the each monk. *Cf. Indian Historical Quarterly*, Vol. XXII, pp. n8.
17. Puṣhyamitraśunga performed two horse sacrifices, they also prove the revival of the Brāhmanical sacrificial cult involving the slaughter of animals which was put down by Aśoka. The Nānāghat inscription of Nāganikā gives a long list of Vedic Sacrifices performed by her husband. They include one Rājasūya and two Aśvamedhas and several other sacrifices such as Ajñyṭādheya, Anārambhanīya, Angirasāturātra, Saptadasātirātra etc. Nearly 21 sacrifices were performed by Sātakarṇi I. Another Sātavāhana king Gautamīputra Sātakarṇi took the title Ēkabrāhmaṇa, Āgama nilaya, The Nasik inscription of Bālasrī shows their leanings towards Bhāgavatism.
18. *Cf. Memoirs of Archaeological Survey of India*, no. 54, p. 6.
19. Kimura, *op.cit.*, p. 40.
20. Daisaku Ikeda, - *Buddhism in the first Millenium*, (Tokyo, Kodenesha International, 1977), p. 84.
21. N.Dutt, *Age of Imperial Unity*, p. 379.
22. Hermann Oldenberg, - *Dīpavaṃsa*, (New Delhi, 1982), pp. 137-140.
23. De La Valle Poussin, “The five points of Mahādeva and the Kathāvatthu”, *Journal of Royal Asiatic Society*, (London, 1910), pp. 413-23.
24. *Cullavagga*, Pali Text Society, Vol. XII, 1.1.
25. P.V. Bapat (ed.) 2500 *Years of Buddhism*, (Delhi, 1960), p. 100.
26. *Ibid*, p. 99.
27. *Ibid*, p. 100.

28. S.Beal, *Buddhist Records of the Western World*, -Vol. II, (Delhi 1983), pp. 164-165.
29. R.Kimura, op. cit, p. 12.
30. *Ibid*, p. 46.
31. *Ibid*, pp. 124-125.
32. *Ibid*, pp. 69-116.
33. Sir Charles Eliot, op. cit, Vol.-II, p. 2.
34. Edward Conze (tr.) *The Largest Sūtra on perfect Wisdom*, (Delhi, 1979), p. 182.
35. M.Winternitz, *History of Indian Literature*, Vol.II, (Delhi, 1978), p. 201.
36. B.S.L.Hanumantha Rao, "The Contemporaneity of Kanishka and Ācarya Nāgārjuna examined", Journal of Āndhra Historical Research Society, Vol.XXVI, (Rajahmundry), pp. 23-24.
37. E.H. Johnston (tr) *Buddhacarita of Aśvaghoṣa* (Delhi, 1978), Introduction, p. XXVI.
37. Cowel, *Buddhacharita*, - p. 148.
38. R.Kimura, op. cit, p. 162.
39. *Ibid*.
40. *Ibid*, p. 143.
41. Michael Hahn, (Ed.) *Nāgārjuna's Ratnāvalī*, vol.I, the basic texts, (Bon, 1982), Chapter-IV, p. 70.
42. *Ibid*, p. 78.
43. *Ibid*, p. 68.
44. R.Kimura, op. cit, p. 84.
45. *Ibid*, pp. 166-167.
46. *Ibid*, p. 185.
47. B.L.Suzuki, *Mahāyāna Buddhism*, (London, 1981), p. 31.
48. R.Kimura, op. cit, p. 176.
49. Nalinaksha Dutt, *Mahāyāna Buddhism*, (Delhi, 1978), p. 141.
50. Jayadev Singh, *An Introduction to Mādhyamika Philosophy*, (Delhi, 1978), p35.
51. B.L.Suzuki, op. cit, p. 34.
52. Jayadev Singh, op. cit, p. 35.
53. R.Kimura, op. cit, pp. 19-20.
54. B.L.Suzuki, op. cit, p. 22.
55. Sir Charles Eliot, op. cit, p. 26.
56. H.Kern and B.Nanjio (Ed.) *Saddharma Pundarīka* (St.Petersburg,

1912) VII, p. 31, quoted by Har Dayal in his Bodhisattva Doctrine in Buddhist Sanskrit Literature.

57. Max Muller and B.Nanjio (Ed.), *Sukhāvatī Vyūha*, (Oxford, 1883), pp. 18-19.
58. *Saddharma Pundarīka*, op. cit, XIV.
59. N.Dutt, "The doctrine of Kāya in Hīnayāna and Mahāyāna," I.H.Q., vol.V, (London), pp. 516-546.
60. Sir Charles Eliot, op. cit, p. 26.
61. N.Dutt op. cit, p. 518.
62. Jayadev Singh, op. cit, p. 47.
63. N.Dutt, op. cit, pp. 518-546.
64. D.T.Suzuki, *Outlines of Mahāyāna Buddhism*, (London, 1907), pp. 266-270.
65. *Ibid.*
66. Hardayal, *The Bodhisattva doctrine in Buddhist Sanskrit Literature*, (Delhi, 1978), reprint, p. 43.
67. B.C.Law, *Studies in the Mahāvastu*, (Delhi, 1978) pp. 21-40.
68. Winternitz, op. cit, p. 249.
69. de La Valle Poussin, The Bodhisattva Doctrine, E.R.E. Vol.II, pp. 739-53.
70. *Ibid.*
71. Sir Charles Eliot, op. cit, p. 7.
72. ERE Vol.V, p. 450.
73. D.T.Suzuki, op. cit, p. 277.
74. Edward Conze, 30 *years of Buddhist Studies*, (London, 1967), p. 68.
75. Sangharakshita (Ed.), *Eternal Legacy*, (London, 1985), Vimalakīrti's Discourse on Emancipation, pp. 164-165.
76. Har Dayal, op. cit, p. 165.
77. Edward Conze, *A Short History of Buddhism*, (London, 1981), XIII, p. 50.
78. Richard Robinson, *Chinese Buddhist Verse*, (London, 1954), p. 22.
79. De La Valle Poussin, E.R.E. Vol. VIII, p. 336.
80. E.R.E. Vol.II, p. 748.
81. N. Dutt, in *The History and Culture of the Indian People*, (Classical Age), Vol.III, (Bombay, 1970), pp. 379-380.
82. E.R.E. Vol.VIII, pp. 336-337.
83. *Ibid.*

84. N.Dutt in *The Age of Imperial Unity*, (Bombay, 1968), IVth Edition, p. 385.
85. C. Bendall, (Ed.) *Santideva's Śikṣā Samuccaya*, (Petersburg, 1897-1902), p. 311.
86. *Ibid*, 318-22.
87. *Ibid*, 312.
88. H. Kern, *Mannual of Indian Buddhism*, (Delhi, 1972), p. 124.
89. N. Dutt, in *Classical Age*, pp. 374-375.
90. *Epigraphia Indica,* Vol.XX, Nāgārjuna konda Inscriptions, No. F. p. 22.
91. Amarasimha, *Amarakośa* (Bombay, 1911).
92. Albert Schwitzer, *Indian Thought and its Development*, (Tr.) by Mrs. C.E.B. Russel (London 1951) Reprint. He quotes from Der Mahāyāna Buddhismus of M.Winternitz.
93. *Bodicaryāvatāra*, (3, 6), quoted by Haripada Chakraborthy in *Asceticism in Ancient India Brāhmanical Buddhist and Jain*, (Calcutta, 1973), p. 31.
94. Sangharaksita (ed.) *Eternal Legacy*, (London, 1985), p. 151.
95. Robert A.F. Thurman, (Tr.) *The Holy Teaching of Vimalakīrti*, (London, 1976), pp. 234-235.
96. L.M. Joshi, *Studies in the Buddhistic Culture of India*, (Delhi, 1967), p. 32.
97. K.Satchidananda Murty, "Āndhra Contribution to Buddhist Thought," N.H. Samtani and H.S. Prasad (ed) Amala Prajna, Aspects of Buddhist Studies, Prof. P.V. Bapat Felicitation Volume (Delhi, 1990).
98. T.R.V.Murty, The *Central Philosophy of Buddhism*, (London, 1980), pp. 5-6.

CHAPTER - II

ORIGINAL HOME OF MAHĀYĀNA BUDDHISM

There is difference of opinion among scholars regarding the origin of Mahāyāna and the conditions under which it evolved.

NORTH-WESTERN ORIGIN

A strong view is that Mahāyānism originated in the north-western region or in the Gāndhāra. This view is based upon the following points:

1. The Western scholars like Max Muller, [1] De La Valle Poussin[2] and A.B.Keith[3] held the view that devotion which is one of the features of Mahāyānism was the result of Western influence. In their opinion Bhakti in Indian religious systems was the result of the impact of Western, particularly the Magdian religion. As Western influence was predominant in the north-west, they held that Mahāyāna was born in those regions.A.B.Keith says that "The sudden activity of Mahāyāna, its conviction of the necessity of the preaching of salvation and the doctrine of the duty of man lay aside the dream of swift release from the transmigration for himself and to choose instead the career of a Buddha to be for the sake of the release of the world from tribulation suggest the introduction of

a new spirit which India was eager and able to assimilate, but which would not have arisen in such a form unless there had been external influences at work."[4]

Some other scholars hold the view that the rise of Mahāyāna Buddhism was the result of the impact of Bhāgavatism. Bhāgavatism originated during the 6th century B.C.[5] Its place of origin was north-western India, that is the kingdom of Śūrasena with its capital at Mathura. Vāsudeva Kṛṣṇa of the *Chāndogya upanishad* was the propounder of Bhāgavatism and therefore it is also called the Vāsudeva cult.[6] Devotion and worship of Bhagavan is the cardinal feature of the Vāsudeva cult. But by about the 2nd C.B.C., Bhāgavatism made rapid progress and became popular. The Śungas who overthrew the Mauryas were Bhāgavatas[7] and even the Indo-Bactrians preferred the system.[8] Therefore, it is argued that as a result of the interaction between Buddhism and Bhāgavatism, Mahāyānism developed in the Nort-Western India. The exponents of this theory think that the concept of Bhakti was borrowed by the Buddhists from Bhāgavadgītā[9] which is the most important authority of the Bhāgavatas.

The above view derives further support from the theory that the probable home of Buddha image was in the North-West. Worship of the image of Buddha is one of the important features of Mahāyānism. It is held by some scholars that Buddhism sprang up against the uniconic Vedic religion[10] and the worship of idols among the Indians was the result of the Perso-Hellenic influence.[11] The first image of Buddha, according to them was produced by the Hellenistic artists in north-western India, especially Gāndhāra.[12] Therefore north-western India was the probable home of Mahāyāna.

Another point that is taken to support the above theory is the assumption that Kanishka was a patron of Mahāyānism.[13] Kanishka ruled north-western India with Puruṣapura as his capital. He is believed to have convened the fourth Buddhist council at Jallundhar.[14]

Even some of the recent writers[15] think that the fourth Buddhist Council was a Mahāyāna Council and Kanishka helped the spread of Mahāyāna system far and wide.

The inevitable conclusion from the above points is that Mahāyāna originated in north-western India. But this theory of north-western origin of Mahāyāna is not convincing for several reasons. The points on which it is based do not stand critical examination:

1. It is not possible to accept the view of the Western scholars like Max Muller, De La Vallee Poussin Louise and others that devotion in the Indian religious systems was the result of Persian influence. In fact, religion without an element of devotion is inconceivable. Even in the highly ritualistic Brāhmanical religion scholars find devotion.[16] Many of the hymns addressed to Indra and Varuṇa were inspired by love and admiration, which are the constituents of Bhakti. For any person who believes in religion, devotion is a psychological necessity. E.J.Thomas says, "Religious devotion is a psychological phenomenon. It is a natural tendency of the soul to seek an object of religious love and worship, and it appears in any state of society, when a suitable object for its exercise appears or is conceived. Even Buddhists sought the object of worship. They found it in the Buddhas and Bodhisattvas, who became little else than the gods of old polytheism, under other names."[17] Even A.B. Keith admits "the seeds of Mahāyānism were in the religious tradition, indigenous to India."[18] Therefore it is not

necessary to trace devotion in Indian religions to Western influence.

Buddhism and Bhāgavatism emerged simultaneously in the eastern and in the north-western parts of India respectively. Bhāgavatism also is believed to have risen as a reaction against the overgrowth of ritualism in Vedic religion.[19] The founder of Bhāgavatism was also a Kṣatriya. Bhāgavatism laid emphasis on *satya, sīla, dāna, niyama, ārjava, ahiṁsa* and other such practical ethical values.[20] In a short time, Vāsudēva Kṛṣṇa, the prophet of Bhāgavatism was deified and came to be worshipped. Gradually he was identified with one of the great Gods of the Brāhmanical pantheon, Nārāyana Viṣṇu.[21] The Bhāgavadgītā became the authority on Bhāgavatism. It is attributed to Vāsudēva Kṛṣṇa and in it the concept of Bhakti has received clear exposition. But the same concept is founḍ in the *Dhammapada* also. There is therefore the possibility of one influencing the other and scholars are divided about the dates of *Bhāgavadgītā* and *Dhammapada*. S.R. Goyal says "the vexed question of literary chronology makes it impossible to determine as to which was the borrower side"[22]. Different writers give different dates to the Gītā. A.D.I. Hill assigns the 2nd C.B.C. as the date of the Gītā[23]. Garbe puts it between 200 B.C. and 200 A.D.[24]. John Webers thinks that it cannot be referred to a period earlier than the 3rd C.A.D.[25] K.T.Telang thinks "the latest date at which the Gītā can have been composed must be earlier than the 3rd C.B.C.[26] Radhakrishnan says that the original text must be assigned to 5th C.B.C. Radhakrishnan assigns the date 500 B.C. to Bhāgavadgītā probably because the founder of Bhāgavatism, Vāsudeva lived about that time. But the renowned scholar himself admits that the Bhāgavadgītā was subjected to interpolations and alterations at several times, [27] It is not possible therefore to ascertain when it has taken the present form.

On the other hand, K.N.Upadhyaya establishes the profound influence of early Buddhism, especially the Nikāyas on *Bhāgavadgītā*[28]. He points out that the Gītā uses certain words such as nirvāṇa, adveṣa, karma, maitrī, rāga and dvesa which do not find place in the Upanishads. In their usage, he finds close resemblance bet-ween *Dhammapada and Gītā* and says, "these similarities of expressions and ideas are ample indication to the fact that the Gītā had assimilated all those Buddhistic elements which it found convenient to fit into its scheme.

Hultzch after making a comparative study of the Edicts of Aśoka and the *Dhammapada* comes to the conclusion that Aśoka's Dhamma was influenced by the *Dhammapada* and his edicts are framed on its model.[29] Therefore the *Dhammapada* must have existed before 250 B.C. and hence there is every possibility that the *Dhammapada* is older than the *Bhāgavadgītā*.

Therefore it is not safe to conclude that the concept of Bhakti was borrowed from the Bhāgavatas or the Persians by the Buddhists. A.B.Keith says : "There existed in India itself partly even in early Buddhism the germs of the results which are revealed in Mahāyāna. We cannot deny that these seeds may have been stirred to active life by the intellectual ferment which must have been caused by the introduction of new peoples to India."[30] There is a tendency on the part of the people to deify a religious teacher. As the Bhāgavatas deified Vāsudeva who was only a teacher, the Buddhists deified the Buddha, the Tathāgata.

In fact in Indian literature, the word *Bhakti* first appeared in the *Therīgāthā,* assigned to the 3rd C.B.C. It speaks of *Bhakti* as follows.[31] *So bhattimā nāme capoti paṇḍitō ñatvā ca dhammesu visesiassa.*" Even in the ancient Pāli *Nikāyas,*[32] the idea of Bhakti is found. It was called *Saddha* (*śraddha*) in the 5th C.B.C. But the word *Saddha* is used to mean faith in the Buddha and is repeatedly declared to be essential for the spiritual development of monks and laymen. On Saddha, *Majjimanikāya* refer to *'Saddhā vimutta'.* Caṅkisutta speaks of *'Saddhā bahukārā'.* It is found in *Dhammapada* as *Sukhā Saddhā patiṭṭhitā.*[33] *Dhammasaṅganī* says 'Saddhā O Kappanā Abhippasādo;. In the words of Hardayal the idea of Bhakti was therefore not a borrowed feather with which Buddhism adorned itself.[34] It has been an integral part of the Buddhist ideal from the earliest times.

Then it is not reasonable to describe the religious systems in India before the rise of Buddhism as all uniconic. The Vedic religion might have been uniconic but that did not form the entire background of Buddhism. There were other indigenous non-Āryan religious systems, which existed side by side with the Vedic system. Magadha, where the new religions sprang up was not yet thoroughly Āryanised by the 6th Century B.C.[35] The primitive religions consisted of the worship of Mother Goddess, Trees, Yakṣas and Nāgas[36] and these systems cannot be said to have been devoid either of devotion or of worship of some object. It is not out of place to mention that the tradition of icon-worship in India was coming down from the Harappan times.[37]

Buddhism developed therefore against a complex religious background. Scholars like H. Jacobi are of the view that 'Buddhism and Jainism attempted at a synthesis of Vedic and Non-Vedic religious principles and practices". According to A.L. Basham "Buddhism sprang up against the primitive animistic background.[38]

There are in fact literary and inscriptional references which point to the existence of the images long before the image of Buddha were supposed to have been produced in Gāndhāra about 1st Century B.C. The Hathigumpha inscription of Khāravela mentions that Mahāpadmananda (400 B.C.) invaded Kalinga and carried away as trophies the images of Jina from Kalinga which Khāravela brought back to his capital.[40] The kingdom of Kalinga at that time extended upto the mouths of the river Godavari on the east-coast.

Niharanjan Ray says : "The human figure which came later on to be the main exponent of Indian art of the classical and early medieval periods considered from this point of view appears to be the gift of un-Āryan southerns of India."[41]

Recently at Parkham, certain Jaina images were discovered. Art critiques assign them to the Mauryan period (320-280 B.C)[42] The *Mahābhāṣya* of Patañjali mentions, that images of Śiva and Viśākha were sold in the streets of Pāṭalīputra.[43] In the *Arthaśāstra of Kautilya* are found references to images and image worship.[44] Therefore the view that the tradition of image-making was imported into India by Perso-Hellenistic rulers of the North-western India and : it proved to be one of the causes for the rise of Mahāyāna does not stand the critical examination.

The theory that Kanishka patronised Mahāyānism also is not correct. During the time of Kanishka, in the north-western India Sarvāstivāda was prevalent. The fourth Buddhist council which is believed to have been summoned by Kanishka was dominated by the Sarvāstivādins.[45] Sarvāstivāda was a branch of Theravāda. Sarvāstivāda no doubt believed in *pudgalaśūnyatā.* But at the same time they believed in the existence of *svabhāva,* the *astitva*. But the Mahāyānists rejected even the existence of *svabhāva*. Their cardinal principle is *sarvaṁ sūnyaṁ*. Therefore most of the criticism of the Mahāyāna philosophers like Nāgarjuna was directed against Sarvastivādins.[46]

Though Aśvaghoṣa, the court poet of Kanishka[47] used the word Mahāyāna, he did not use the term in the sense that it was a separate system.[48] He used the word Mahāyāna for Buddhism itself as the religion of the perfect one.

So the theory of the origin of Mahāyāna in the north-western region stands on weak foundations and hence unconvincing.

ORISSA THEORY

N.K.Sahu propounded the theory that Orissa was the original home of Mahāyāna.[49] He bases his theory on a statement of Lama Tārānātha, the Tibetan historian of Indian Buddhism. Tārānātha lived during the 18th century A.D. Tārānātha wrote that Mahāyāna teachings were originated in the East by Sthavira Arhat Nanda of Aṅga.[50] Further, Sahu derives support to his theory from the statement of *Prajñā-Pāramitā*.[51] According to it, Mañjuśrī Bodhisattva visited Oḍivisa, evidently Orissa and presented a text to its king[52]. The text is taken to be the *prajñā-pāramitā* itself. Sahu further argues that the Mahāsāṅghikas of Āndhra were very orthodox and radical concepts such as *advaya* and *śūnyatā* can not be attributed to them.

The theory of Sahu also is very weak and does not stand the test of critical examination:

(1) In the first place, the testimony of Tārānātha who lived and wrote during the 18th century cannot be accepted without any independent and reliable piece of

corroborative evidence. No other authority supports the view that Aṅga was the birth place of Mahāyāna.

(2) Further, Tārānātha states that Mañjuśrī visited Odivisa and presented a Text to her king. The statement cannot be interpreted that the Text had been composed in Oḍivisa itself. Mañjuśrī brought it from somewhere else and hence Orissa was not its birth place.

(3) Moreover it is not certain that the text was *prajñā-Pāramitā.* There is a difference of opinion among the Buddhists regarding the nature of the book presented to the king. The Sautrāntikas think that it was *Aṣṭasāhasrika Prajñā pāramitā* whereas the Tāntrikas hold the view that it was *Tattva Sangraha.*[53] Therefore, the theory of Sahu is based upon the questionable identification of the Book with *prajñā-Pāramitā.*

(4) It may be recalled that the Andhakas or the Mahāsāṅghikas of Āndhra were in the forefront of all the movements of reform as evidenced by the discussions in the third Buddhist Council, [54] compiled in the *Kathāvatthu* and therefore the argument of Sahu that the Andhakas were rigidly orthodox cannot be sustained.

(5) According to an important Mahāyāna work, *Gaṇḍavyūha,* Mañjuśrī made Dhānyakaṭaka his seat and converted many Nāgas around that place.[55] It is therefore clear that Mañjuśrī presented the book to the king of Orissa which he had brought from Dhānyakaṭaka. Further the *Prajñā-Pāramitā* itself states that Mahāyāna would be born in the south, migrate to the east and flourish in the north.[56] The Mahāyāna texts *Prajñā-Pāramitā* and *Gaṇḍavyūha* thus contradict the account of Tārānātha on which Sahu has based his theory.

(6) The chinese traveller, Yuan Chwang writes that

in Orissa the monks studied Hīnayāna and hated Mahāyānists as 'sky flower-heritics as bad as Kāpālikas.'[57] Orissa, therefore cannot be accepted as the birth place of Mahāyāna.

THEORY OF ĀNDHRA ORIGIN

The avilable literary and archaeological evidence point to Āndhradēśa as the more probable home of Mahāyāna. The socio-economic as well as the religious conditions in Āndhra during the early centuries on either side of the Christian era also appear to be very favourable for the rise of Mahāyāna system.

DATE OF ĀNDHRA BUDDHISM

Buddhist sacred works like *Suttanipata*[58] *Vimanavatthu*[59] and *Kathāvatthu*[60] would have us believe that Buddhism entered Āndhradēśa long before the Third Buddhist Council. The 13th Rock Edict of Aśoka says[61] that the Āndhras who were living within the Mauryan empire had already been following the Buddha Dhamma. A few years back, a stele was unearthed at Amaravati and commenting on it, A.Ghosh and H. Sircar remark that the early phase of 'Amaravati sculpture was earlier than that of Sanchi[62]. Recently a fragment of Āsokan pillar has been discovered at Dhanyakataka and the portion of the edict on it resembles the Girnar edict. D.C.Sircar, who edited the record had expressed the view that the stupa at the place might have been built by Āsoka himself.[63] The recent excavations at the site of Amaravati stupa suggest that Āsoka rebuilt and enlarged the already existing stupa and provided it with a granite railing.[64] On some of these granites is found the polish typical of the Mauryan period.

The label inscriptions on the granites are in Mauryan characters.[65] Even on the Bhaṭṭiprolu stone receptacles are found Mauryan polish[66] and inscriptions in Mauryan characters.[67] Therefore, it may be concluded that Buddhism entered Āndhradēśa even earlier than the Third Buddhist Council of Aśoka.

ĀNDHRA AT THE TIME OF ADVENT OF BUDDHISM

About the time of the advent of Buddhism, the socio-economic and religious conditions in Āndhra were favourable not only for the rapid spread of the religion but also for its development on new lines.

SOCIO-ECONOMIC CONDITIONS

Most scholars agree that Buddhism had rapidly spread among the non-Aryan peoples.[68] The Āndhras are castigated in the Brāhmanical literature as Mlecchas and deserve to live only outside the villages.[69] The Āndhras were not a single race and they were formed by the union of several tribes like the Yakshas and Nāgas.[70] Particularly the Nāgas were predominant in the Kṛṣṇa valley and the Yakshas and Nāgas, we learn from the Buddhist literature were ardent follwers of Buddhism.[71] The Yeṛragudi edicts of Aśoka give us the impression[72] that the people in the region were not uncivilised or unlettered. In the words of R.K.Mookerji, in his Yeṛragudi edict, "Aśoka seems to be extending here the scope of his preaching of *Dhamma.* He appears to enjoin its preaching among both the civil and military classes and especially among the youth, the student population of the country as its future citizens who should be trained in disciplined life. The teachers are also enlisted by him, along with the administrative officers, the

Mahāmatras, in the work of carrying his *Dhamma* or message to the student population as the appropriate sphere of their work, while the rural welfare officers, the *Rāṣṭrikas* are to work for the same mission in the country-side in their charge."[73] Further if the date 400 B.C. and place, Gōdāvari delta of the great *Sūtrakāra,* Āpastamba, suggested by Buhler[74] and Kane[75] are accepted, we may say that the Brāhmanical socio-religious systems were striking roots in Āndhradēśa by about the time.

The Classical Writers, especially Megasthanese wrote that the Āndhras possessed 30 walled towns and their rulers had a huge army.[76] The *Arthaśāstra* of Kautilya noted that trade with the south was more profitable than with the north-west.[77] The east coast with its fertile Gōdāvari and Kṛṣṇa deltas were producing large quantities of rice.[78] The iron implements and fragments of gold ornaments found in the innumerable Megalithic tombs in Āndhra indicate the good condition of metal industry in the land.[79] Such an economic activity naturally led to urbanisation and the statement of Classical Writers has been attested by the discovery of ruins of Śātavāhana and pre Śatavāhana townships at places like Dhūlikaṭṭa, pedabankur, Koṇḍapur, Gājulabaṇḍa, Dhānyakaṭaka, Bhaṭṭiprolu, Chebrolu, Vijayapuri, Chandavaram, Śātānikota, Vīrāpuram, Ādāpur etc.[80] From early days Āndhradēśa had profitable inland and maritime trade. She exported large quantities of rice and probably cotton fabrics. There were routes connecting the east coast with the west across the plateau.[81] Paithan gained importance because it was at the converging point of routes between the east coast and west and north and south. The *Suttanipata* describes a route leading from Assaka, an Āndhra Janapada to the north.[82] There was an eastern route which Aśoka might have followed in leading his armies against Kalinga. From Patalīputra the route passed through Kosala, Kalinga and reached the mouths of the Kṛṣṇa (Maisolia) where from it branched off - one branch going direct southwards to Kanchi and the other proceeding westwards reached Banavāsi in Mysore.[83]

The Prakrit inscriptions of Guṇṭupalli[84] and Ghaṇṭa-śala[85] of the Ikṣvāku times mention Mahānavikas. The ship marked coins of later Śatavāhanas are a clear proof of the encouragement they gave to the maritime trade.[86] The Roman gold coins[87] discovered at many places in Āndhra suggest that maritime trade was profitable. The flourishing condition of agriculture, industry and trade had enriched the *Gahapati* (peasant land-lords), *Karmakara* (artisans) and seṭṭi (merchant) sections of people, who formed the back-bone of Buddhism. Most of the Buddhist Kṣetras were situated by the side of the centres of industry and trade or on important trade routes. Longhurst, who excavated Nāgārjunakoṇḍa remarks that "The devotees of the good law were largely recruited from the commercial classes and it was their wealth which enabled not only the merchants themselves but also their royal masters to raise monuments of such magnificence as those at Nāgārjunakoṇda and at Amarāvatī."[88] it is interesting to note that Āndhra sculpture has some urbanity. The Āndhra sculpture reflects the luxuriant life led by its Patrons, the rich artisan and merchant classes. By that time Mahāyāna system was already in formation. Niharanjan Ray remarks that "Amaravati and other cognate sites in the Kṛṣṇa valley on the other hand lay within easy reach of the rich coastal ports, a few of which at least sheltered Roman trading settlements. The reliefs of the Kṛṣṇa valley particularly of Amaravati, thus naturally reflects the disposition and attitude of urban trading communities which usually manifests preference for a quickened tempo of life. pleasures of the senses, exuberant expression of Joy and passion and for bourgeois elegance and sophistication."[89]

RELIGIOUS CONDITIONS

Like all primitive peoples, the Āndhras during early times appear to have practised animism.[90] Animism is belief in spiritual beings. Tree and animal worship is a part of Animism and this might have led to the worship of Yakshas. It was believed that Yakshas dwelt in trees. One of the early inscriptions of Amaravati contains the statement "*Yaksha Chandramukho vakula vasina*" which means Yaksha by name Chandramukha resides in *vakula tree*.[91] One of the tribes that had gone into the making of the Āndhra race is believed to be Yakshas.[92] According to A.K.Coomaraswamy the Yakshas were great builders.[93] There are several references in the *Mahāvaṁsa* to the belief that one becomes Yaksha after death.[94] Caityas and Ayatanas were built where such Yakshas were worshipped.[95] It is not improbable that the worship of ancestors was prevalent among the Yaksha tribe which developed into the belief in the existence of divine Yakshas and it led naturally to the worship of Yakshas.

Archaeological evidence points to the existence of Megalithic culture among the early people of Āndhradēśa.[96] Throughout Āndhra with the exception of the Coastal region, north of the Godavari, numerous megalithic burials were discovered. The religious significance of Megalithic culture is that it indicates belief in life after death and construction of memorials enshrining the remains of the deceased. Veneration of the bodily remains of the deceased elders was not thus new to the

Āndhras. Most of the archaeologists share the view that the Stupa or Caitya architecture developed from that of the Megalithic cairn circle[97] and it is amply proved by the recently discovered Stupa on the hill near the village of Vaḍḍamānu.[98] At Amaravati[99] and Nāgārjunakoṇḍa[100] Megaliths are found below some of the stupas. With the introduction of Buddhism, it appears that the old Megalithic culture received a new dimension and significance. Many scholars believe that the Caityaka sect was the direct out-growth of the Megalithic beliefs and practices.[101]

In addition, the early Āndhras worshipped Mother Goddess.[102] Several terracotta images of Mother Goddess were found at Koṇḍapur. In fact she is the (mostancient) oldest diety that was worshipped by man all over the world.

The practices of such as the worship of trees and animals, Yakshas and building āyatanas and Caityas for them, and the Megalithic burrials indicate clearly that the iconic devotion was prevalent among the Āndhras. D.C.Sircar says that the concept of *Bhakti* was probably borrowed along with other ideas by the Aryans from the pre-Aryan religious beliefs.[103]

BRĀHMANISM

Against the background of such primitive non-Aryan beliefs and practices Brāhmanism entered Āndhradeśa. The *Sūtras* of Āpastamba reveal that by his time in Āndhradēśa, Brāhmanism made considerable progress.[104] Śatakarṇi I, the third Śātavāhana king who was called *Dakshinapadhapati* performed numerous Vedic sacrifices[105] which are a clear proof of the condition of Brāhmanism.

But Brāhmanism was already undergoing a radical change. The very Nānāghat inscription of Nāgānika which describes the various sacrifices of Śatakarṇi, records that change.[106] It begins with the invocation of the gods of the *Bhakti* cult, Sankarṣaṇa and Vāsudeva, which is a clear evidence of compromise between the ritualism of early Brāhmanism and Vāsudeva Bhāgavatism. Gradually Bhāgavatism became popular in the Deccan. The name of the very second king of the Śatavāhana dynasty, Kanha (Kṛṣṇa) is an evidence of the popularity of Vāsudeva cult among the Śatavāhanas.[107]

One of the hills in Western India is called Kanhagiri (Kṛṣṇagiri).[107-a] In the inscriptions of Western Indian caves we come across the names of donors such as Viṣnu-kuṇḍin,[108] Kṛṣṇa,[109] Viṣnuka,[110] Sudarśana,[111] Viṣnu-pālita[112] etc., which are all Vaiṣnavite and indicate the prevelence of Vāsudēva cult. Thus it appears that Bhāgavatism entered Deccan and trickled down to the South and under the aegis of the Śatavāhanas a compromise was effected between Bhāgavatism, Brāhmanism and Neo-Brāhmanism or Puranic theism. Grierson remarks that Bhāgavatism became popular because of the struggle for life and death between Brāhmanism and Buddhism. In order to combat the purely atheistic Buddhism, the pantheistic Brāhmanists won over to their side the monotheistic Bhāgavatas and the price they paid was the identification of Vāsudeva with Viṣnu of their pantheon".[113] Charles Eliot praises the wisdom of the Brāhmanas in making such compromises. He says : "In critical and revolutionary times, the Brāhmins have often assured their pre-eminence by the judicious recognition of heresies. In all ages, there has been a conservative clique which restricted religion to ceremonial observances. Again and again, some intellectual or emotional outburst has swept away such narrow limits and proclaimed doctrines which seemed subversive of orthodoxy of the day. But they have simply become orthodoxy of the morrow, under the protection of the same Brāhmin caste. The assailants are turned into champions in time, the bold reformers stiffen into antiquated saints".[114] The new religion is characterised by fervent devotion to a personal god, either Viṣnu or Śiva, performance of *vrata, dāna* and pilgrimage. The Śuṅgas in the North and the Śatavāhanas in the South appear to have been great champions of this neo-Brāhmanism. Even the foreigners like the Indo-Bactrians could find their pagan gods in Viṣnu and Śiva, and they were attracted towards Vaiṣṇavism and Śaivism.[115] The Greek ambassador to the Court of the Śuṅgas, Heliodorus set up a *garuḍa* pillar at Besnagar.[116]

ŚAIVISM

About the same time Śiva also appears to have been admitted into the pantheon of Āryan gods and was identified with Vedic Rudra. In Deccan and South India Śiva was worshipped from ancient times. The tridents found in the Megalithic burrials led archaeologists like Alchin to the view that those people worshipped Śiva.[117] Patanjali mentions Śiva Bhāgavatas.[118] The Liṅga of Guḍimallam and the tradition recorded in the inscription[119] of Śthanakuṇḍur reveal that some of the early Śātavāhana kings were devoted to Śiva. Art critics assign the Guḍimallam Mukhaliṅga to the 2nd cenurty B.C.[120] and the human form of Śiva on the Liṅga resembles a *niśāda*.[121] It indicates that Śiva was originally the god of non-Āryans.

Gradually puranic theism or neo-Brāhmanism was developed and much literature was produced. The *Gāthāsaptaśatī*[122] whose compilation is attributed to king Hala, the 17th king in the Śatavāhana dynasty, contains *Gāthas*, with Śaivite and Vaiṣṇavite themes. Gautamiputra Śātakarṇi is compared in the Nasik inscription[123] to many Puraṇic heroes and is described as *āgamānāṁ nilaya* (the abode of agamas) which may be Puraṇic literature. The picturesque mythology of the purāṇas also was intended to popularise neo-Brāhmanism.

BUDDHISM

Buddhism, which had already made considerable progress in Āndhradēśa naturally reacted to the developments taking place in Brāhmanical religion. The Andhakas as the Āndhra Buddhists were known in the early days appear to have been in the forefront of all the later developments in Buddhism. They were probably the first to realise the need to reform their own religion to meet the challenge of neo-Brāhmanism and started to study afresh the teachings of the Buddha to bring out their deeper meanings, under the leadership probably of Mahādēva. In the Second Council held at Vaiśāli the saṅgha broke up into the Theravada and Mahāsaṅghika schools.[124] It was a revolt against the rigid orthodoxy which refused to allow any change in the discipline. One strong view is that the great split occured in the Saṅgha on the issue of the five principles of Mahādēva, [125] which also might have been the results of the discussions carried on by the Andhakas. The main issues were :

1. An *Arhat* may have doubts on matters of doctrine;
2. One cannot attain arhat hood without the help of a preceptor;

3. One may be an *Arhat* and may not know it;
4. An *Arhat* may commit sin under unconscious temptations;
5. The noble way may be gained by a shout.

This Mahādeva who propounded these principles cannot be the same as the one whom Aśoka sent to Mahiṣamaṇḍala. The former should have lived much earlier, and there is every reason to believe that he resided in Āndhradeśa, at Dhānyakaṭaka.

After the second Council, Āndhradēśa became a great centre of the Mahāsaṅghikas.[126] No doubt the word Mahāsaṅghika does not occur in the inscriptions of Āndhradēśa. But there is plenty of evidence in support of the view that the Mahāsaṅghikas were strong in Āndhra: (1) In several inscriptions we come across the words like *Ariya Haghana,*[127] *Ārya Saṁgham,*[128] *Ārya Saṅghasa.*[129] The word *Ārya,* is generally used as a synonym of *Mahā* and hence *Āryasaṅgha* of the records should be taken to mean Mahāsaṅgha.[130] (2) An inscription from Dhānyakaṭaka states;[131] "*Hamghi gahapati putasa dusakasa*" which means that Dusaka who was a member of the saṅgha was a lay worshipper. It was the Mahāsaṅghika school that admitted the lay worshippers into the Saṅgha. Lay worshippers had no place in Theravada Saṅgha. It is therefore clear that Dusaka was a Mahāsaṅghika Buddhist. The inscription makes it clear that the Mahāsaṅghikas were present at Dhānyakaṭaka. (3) An inscription from Nāgārjunakoṇḍa mentions[132] *Digha Majjima Nikāya dhara* and *Pancamaṭika dhara.* The *Abhidhamma* was known originally as *Matika (Māṭrkā),* which term later came to be used for both *Vinaya* and *Abhidhamma.* The Mahāśaṅghikas had their own *Vinaya* and *Abhidhamma.* Their *Vinaya* was in five parts the *Vinaya* is generally mentioned after the *Nikāyas* and therefore the term *Pancamātika*[133] refers to the *Vinaya* of the Mahāsaṅghikas, who were evidently present at Dhānyakaṭaka and Śrīparvata.

Āndhradēśa was not merely the stronghold of the Mahāśaṅghika system but it may be the very birth place of the system, if it is accepted that the five principles of Mahādeva were responsible for its rise. There is every reason to believe that the Bhikkhu was lived on at Dhānyakaṭaka. Mahādeva is said to have been a resident of *Caityaśaila*[134] which can satisfactorily be identified with Dhānyakaṭaka. A large number of inscriptions from Dhānyakaṭaka contain the word *Caityaka* in its different forms: *Cetikiya, Cetika, Cetiyavaṁdaka, Jetikiya* and *Catiyavadaka*. But the later inscriptions of Dhānyakaṭaka contains only the term *Seliya* nam and therefore it is clear that the term '*Sailiya*' replaced '*Caityaka*'.

One of the Rāmatirtham seals refers to 'Śelasaghasa'[141] and therefore it may be concluded that the Caityakas were also known as Śeliyas. The Śailas or Caityakas branched off into Pūrvaśailas and Aparāśailas and Amaravati became the seat of the Pūrvaśaila.[142] Vasumitra used the words Caitya Śaila and Aparaśaila[143] for which Vinitideva used the words Pūrvaśaila and Aparaśaila.[144] It is evident therefore that the early writers used the terms Pubbasela or Purva Śaila and Caityaśaila as synonyms. The *Kathāvatthu* attributes the five principles of Mahādeva to the Pūrvaśailas.[145] Therefore Pubbasela was identical with Caityaśaila. This clearly indicates that Dhānyakaṭaka was known even as Caityaśaila and it was the place where Mahādeva lived. Hence, Dhānyakaṭaka was the birth place of the five principles, which led to the great schism in the Saṅgha and the emergence of the Mahāsaṅghikas.

PRINCIPLES AND PRACTICES OF THE CAITYAKAS

WORSHIP OF CAITYA :—The most striking principle of the Caityakas was the worship of caitya. The name Caityaka appears to be the result of their intimate association with Caitya.[146] The Caityakas specialised in the construction of huge caityas resembling Śailas, justifying probably the expressions like Caityaśaila and Caityagiri. They developed the faith that construction, decoration and worship involving circumambulation, offering of garlands, flowers, lights and incense were meritorious acts.[147]

BUDDHA AS LOKOTTARA:—The Caityakas started worshipping the Caitya because it generally enshrined the *dhātu* of the Buddha whom they conceived as supramundane or *Lōkottara.* They held that the Buddha was free from attachment, ill-will and delusion and was possessed of finer elements. He was far superior to *Arhat* by virtue of having acquired the ten powers. The *Mahāvastu* which describes Buddha as supramundane, above the laws and conditions of ordinary human existence is the *Vinaya* of the Lokottaravādins. The work lays emphasis on Caitya worship. [148] Nalinaksha Dutt therefore concludes that the Caityakas were identical with Lokottaravādins.[149] The word Caityaka is ritualistic or religious whereas the word *Lokottara* is idealogical or philosophical.

ARHAT NOT PERFECT:—Another belief of the Caityakas is that an *Arhat* is not a perfect being.[150] The Caityakas accepted the five points of Mahādeva. They strongly held the view that one cannot become a perfect being without the help of a preceptor,[151] and they replaced the ideal of arhathood by that of Buddhahood.These ideas gradually developed into faith in the grace of Bodhisattva and dependence upon it.

TRANSFER OF MERIT:—Another view held by the Caityakas was that merit one acquires could be transferred to friends and relations and one acquires merit for the welfare of entire mankind.[152] Such a view is possible only when one has realised the fundamental oneness of life. *advaya.*[153] This idea is quite opposed to the original Buddhism which laid emphasis on *attadipa* and *attasaraṇa*[154] that means self-effort.

NIRVĀṆA IS NOT THE GOAL:—The Pūrvaśailas who were a branch of the Caityakas were indifferent to Nirvāṇa. The *Kathāvatthu* says that the Pūrvaśailas held the view that Nirvāṇa is an object of the thought of a person not yet free from bondage.[155] The statement *Nibbānadhātu* is *kuśaia* bears that the implication that the Purvāsailas believed in the postponement of nirvāṇa till the entire mankind is emancipated.[156]

VETULYAKA BELIEFS:—The Vetulyakas were another branch of the Andhakas.[157] Buddhaghosa calls them Mahāśūnytavādins. He has attributed a docetic thesis to this school as found in the *Kathāvatthu.* The Ceylonese chronicles make mention of the Vetulyakas as heretics whom the chroniclers noted at the Abhayagiri monastery in Ceylon.[158] They were also known as Vaipulyas probably because they were either among the authors of the *Vaipulyasūtras* or their system was based upon them.[159] They developed certain metaphysical ideas and religious practices, which cleared the way for Mahāyāna. The Vaitulyakas idealise the notion of the Saṅgha and put it on a spiritual plane, whereas the Theravadins hold that it is an organisation of monks. The two opinions reflect amply upon the two divergent tendencies to which the different sects were pulling powerfully viz., the real and ideal, the rational and the metaphysical, the human and superhuman which ultimately resulted in the crystalisation of the Hīnayana and Mahāyāna."

The Vaitulyakas assert that sexual relations may be entered upon with a unified resolve.[160] They believe in family life and even monks could be permitted to have contact with a woman out of compassion. "We seem to have here more a Mahāyānic than Vajrayānic anticipation".[161] It is interesting to note that in Ceylon the Mahāyānists were known as Vaitulyakas or Vaitulyavādins and they were said to have entered the island from the east coast of India, evidently Āndhradeśa.

The Caityakas thus played a prominent part in developing the doctrine and discipline of Buddhism during its early days and gave practically a new orientation to Buddhism, The five points of Mahādeva which they adopted led them to doubt the system in which each individual strove to become an *Arhat*. The superhuman conception of the Buddha and the introduction of worship transformed a simple code of morals intended for self improvement into a picturesque religion satisfying the religious requirements of the common people. Sukumara Dutt acknowledges the part played by the Andhakas in developing Buddhology.[162] The Caityaka belief in the need of a preceptor led to the growth of Bodhisattva ideal. The Purvāśaila indifference to Nirvāṇa and the Vetulyaka concept of emptiness paved the way for the rise of Mahāyānism based on the Śūnyavāda of Nāgārjuna.

Sukumara Dutt is not correct in stating that there is

no sculptural or epigraphical evidence to the existence of Mahāyān in Āndhra in general and Dhānyakaṭaka in particular.[163] The innumerable inscriptions recovered from places like Dhānyakaṭaka, Nāgārjunakoṇḍa, Bhaṭṭiprolu and Jaggayyapeta clearly give us an idea of the developments in Buddhism which point to the rise of Mahāyān in Āndhradēśa.

EPIGRAPHICAL EVIDENCE

DIVINITY OF BUDDHA:—The inscriptions from Dhānyakaṭaka, Bhaṭṭiprolu, Nāgārjunakoṇḍa and other Buddhist sites reveal the gradual transformation of Buddha from Tathāgata to Bhagavān. The earliest inscriptions begin simply with the word "*Siddhaṁ*".[164] Some others do not contain even that statement. *Siddham* means 'perfect one'. There are several inscriptions which begin with '*namo bhagavato*'[165] while a few others begin with '*Siddham namo bhagavato*'[166] which means 'salutation to the perfect one who is adorable'. The use of the word *Bhagavato* clearly indicates that by that time Buddha was considered as *Bhagavan* by the Andhakas. One record actually contains the statement "*Bhagavato Mahācetiyasa*",[167] which means the Mahācaitya of *Bhagavan*. . In one of the Nāgārjunakoṇḍa inscriptions the pious donor calls the Buddha as '*svamatasya Devasya*'[168] which clearly means 'the god of my religion'. Most of the inscriptions contain statements which reveal supramundane nature of Buddha. The Nāgārjunakoṇḍa inscriptions describe the Buddha as the conqueror of the hosts of Mara, viz., lust, anger, fear, desire, thirst, delusion and hatred (Jita kāma bhaya harisa, Tarisa, mōha, desa, dapita, Mārābala, dapamāna pasamanakarasa).[169] Another inscription describes the Buddha as "cakra lakṣana sukumāra sujāta caraṇēna"[170] as "daśabala mahābala" "the leader of the law of the three worlds and as one honoured by the lord of gods" (Teloka dhamma dhuravahasa, dēvarāja sākatasa).[171] Another inscription describes Buddha as Agapogalasa (The best of all beings).[172] One of the inscriptions describes Buddha as Logāthikāsa[173] (The illuminator of the world). In the Indrapalanagara grant, Buddha is described as dvātriṁśaṅ mahāpuruṣa lakṣaṇa varopa lakṣita.[174] The same Indrapalanagara plates describe the Buddha as Saṁbuddha-highly enlightened and kripātmana (compassionate). The record further attributes to him Daśabala, (Dasabala-mahābala) *Caturvaiśāradya (Caturvaiśaradyaviśārada)* and *aṣṭādaśa aveṇikādharma.*

The ten powers which the Buddha achieved are:

1. Knowledge of what is possible, what is impossible;
2. Knowledge of fruition of action past, present and future;
3. Knowledge of the objectives of all paths;
4. Knowledge of many and varied elements of the world;
5. Knowledge of varied individuals and intentions;
6. Knowledge of the faculties of all beings;
7. Knowledge of purity and impurity and growth of the trances *samādhi*; concentration and attainments;
8. Knowledge of numberless former existences (*Pūrvani vāsaṁvetti)*
9. The divine eye that can see the beings passing away and beings reborn according to their *karma*; and

10. Capacity to destroy the *āsavas*[175]

The four Vaiśāradyas are the Buddha's four "Grounds of Self-confidence". These are:

1. Knowledge that he has attained perfect enlightenment and that he understands all principles and phenomena;
2. Knowledge that he has destroyed all the evils;
3. Knowledge that the obstacles to the higher life which he has described really constitute serious hindrances; and
4. The knowledge that the way which he teaches for the cessation of pain and evil really leads to that goal.[176]

According to the Mahāyānists in attaining the *pāramitas,* Bodhisattva must pass through the ten stages *(dasabhūmis).* In the eighth stage he acquires the above mentioned four confidences or vaiśāradyas.

AVEṆIKA DHARMAS

Āveṇika Dharmas are the special characteristics and they distinguish a Buddha from all other beings.[177]

This triple formula of the *balas, vaiśāradyas* and *āveṇika dharmas* constitutes the stock definition of Buddha in later times.[178] It is therefore quite evident that the Buddhists of Āndhradēśa were quite familiar with the developed form of Mahāyāna canonical literature.

The inscriptions from Bhaṭṭiprolu which are considered as the earliest (200 B.C.) hold the Buddha as almost *Lokottara.* They attributed supernatural powers to the *Dhātus* of the Buddha by stating that *Buddha Sarīrāni Mahāniyāni Sarmaṇe".* [179] The Ayaka pillar inscription from Nāgārjunakoṇḍa describes Buddha, "*Dhātuvara Parigamhitasa*" possessed of excellent *Dhātus).*[180] de La Valle Poussin comments on it that those ideas are the basis for the *Dharmadhātu.*[181] *Dharmadhātu* is a kind of Buddhist Brāhman for the followers of Mahāyāna and from this conception of *Dharmadhātu* emanated the *Trikaya* theory.

At Nāgārjunakoṇḍa several images of Buddha in the round have been found on the lotuses.[182] According to the *Brihatsamhita* "like the Father of the Universe, creator Brahma, the Buddha is to be seated on lotus."[183] In these images the Buddha was therefore conceived as *Ādi Buddha* (the Supreme Lord of the Universe) sending Buddhas and Bodhisattvas into the world.[184]

It may finally be added that the Tummalagudem record lays emphasis on two qualities of the Buddha, namely, *Saṁbodhi* (perfect enlightenment) and *Kripa* (compassion) and it is discussed alone in chapter-1 significance of *Prajñā* and *karuṇā* and their inter-dependence in Mahāyāna. Therefore the record is an incontrovertible evidence to the existence of Mahāyāna in Āndhra.

Sukumara Dutt is therefore not correct in saying that before the visit of Yuan Chwang there is neither inscriptional nor sculptural evidence to the existence of Mahāyāna in Āndhradēśa. The above pieces of evidence clearly reveal how the principles and practices of Mahāyāna originated and developed in Āndhra viharas. In support of this view the following points also may be considered :

DEVOTION AND WORSHIP

According to the available sculptural and epigraphical

evidence the Andhakas worshipped Buddha in the form of symbols till the introduction of the Buddha image around 150 A.D. The symbols that represented the Buddha were the Bodhi Tree, Throne, *Dharmachakra, Triratna, Swastika, Buddhapadas* and *caitya* or *stupa* as revealed by sculptures.[185] From the precious objects such as gold flowers, beads, pearls, gold tridents probably *Triratna* symbols [186] found in association with the *Dhātus* at several places suggest the devotion with which the *Dhātus* were worshipped before they were deposited. In many sculptures[187] from Dhānyakaṭaka and Nāgārjunakoṇḍa we find men and women kneeling before the symbols and the images with folded hands and with forehead touching the ground - a posture suggesting deep devotion or *prapatti,* the concept of complete self-surrender. At Bhaṭṭiprolu by the side of the *Dhātu*, pearls were arranged in the shape of *svastika.*[188] We learn from the sculptures of Amaravati[189] and Nāgārjunakoṇḍa[190] that *swastika* stood for the Buddha. At Bhaṭṭiprolu, Dhānyakaṭaka and Śalihuṇḍam[191] the *Dhātus* were preserved in crystal caskets, the use of which appears to have special significance. It was probably inspired by the account of *Lalitavistara*[192] that Bodhisattva was in a crystal in the womb of Māyā devi.

With the rise of Mahāyāna the symbolic worship was replaced by Buddha image, worship in anthropomorphic form. By about the middle of the 2nd century A.D., the image of Buddha was introduced at Dhānyakaṭaka. In consequence the worship of the image of Buddha became rapidly popular. The images of Buddha were installed in Caitya grihas and at cardinal points of the Stupas and Vihāras. They were not only installed but also the ritual of consecration was developed. It is significant that one of the standing images at Nāgārjunakoṇḍa has a hole between its feet from which pearls, pieces of gold and other precious objects have been recovered.[193] The term *pratiṣṭa* which occurs in the Nāgārjunakoṇḍa[194] and Jaggayyapeṭa[195] inscriptions may also be taken to refer to such a ritual. The images thus consecrated appear to have been decorated with jewels. The Amaravati inscription[196] of the pallava king Simhavarman who visited the Buddha *Kṣetra* about 550 A.D. speaks of jewels wonderfully worked in gems, gold and silver (*maṇi, kanaka, rajita vicitra).* Flowers, lamps, sandal paste and incense were used in the worship and there was *Nitya Naivedya* (offering of daily food)[197]. The Tummalagudem inscription of Vishnukuṇḍin king of the 5th century A.D.[198] records a gift to the Vihara for providing *dīpa, dhūpa, gaṅdha puṣpa, pāna, bhōjana* etc., which constitute *Aṅgabhoga.*

TRANSFER OF MERIT

Many of the inscriptions from Āndhra Buddhist sites record gifts made with the aim of welfare and happiness for the entire mankind *(sarva lōka hita sukha*). The Mahāyānists as noted in chapter I, cultivated a noble selfless social outlook and showed a readiness to share the merit of their gifts and other pious deeds with their relations as well as with the rest of mankind. One inscription from Keśānapalli[199] mentions that the donor Mahārathi Mahāchāma donated a Buddhinikaṁba for the Nirvāṇa of entire mankind, who are fettered by evils. Another inscription mentions[200] that the aim of the gift is Sarvalokahita sukha "for the sake of the welfare and happiness of all sentient beings." Chamtisiri made several gifts with the aim of the attainment of welfare and happiness by all the world.[201] Bodhisiri donated[202] for the universe welfare and happiness of the assembly of saints and that of the whole world. Kodabalisiri[203] donated a monastery with the aim of the welfare and happiness of all sentient beings. Even the orthodox Theravadins at Nāgārjunakoṇḍa appear to have been influenced by the noble concept of the Mahāyānists. The foot-print inscription[204] says that the Mahāvīharavāsins installed the feet of Buddha with a prayer "for the welfare and happiness of all beings". A certain upāsaka Kumaranandi instals an image of Buddha[205] for his own happiness and for the happiness of all the sentient beings. The inscription recording this pious deed ends in true Mahāyāna spirit with the wish that the entire world may attain Nirvāṇa by the merit of the gift (*tena puṇyena lōkoyaṁ Nirvāṇamadhigachatu).*

THE AIM OF RELIGIOUS PRACTICE

Consistent with the theory of Many Buddhas, the Mahāyānists as noted above believed that every one is a potential Buddha. In their view arhathood is not perfect. Any one, either an *Upasaka* or *Bhikku,* by observing religious practices would attain Buddhahood. This idea is clearly expressed in an inscription from Jaggayyapeṭa.[206] According to the record an *Upāsaka* installed an image of Buddha with the hope of attaining Buddhahood *(Buddhatvaprāpti nimittam)* - which is the highest goal of the Great Vehicle. No better evidence is required to prove that by the 4th century A.D., even common people in Āndhra were imbued with the noble spirit of Mahāyāna.

LITERARY EVIDENCE

The Mahāsaṅghikas who had set up their centres in the Kṛṣṇā valley realised, in view of the changed religious situation in the land, the need to bring out the deeper meaning of *Buddhavacanas* and make their religion broad-based so that it could become more agreeable to the people. In their viharas they carried on prolonged discussions, resulting in the compilation of *Vaipulya Śutras* -which mean elaboration of the meaning of *Buddha vacana*. These include *prajñāpāramitā, Ratnakūta,* Avataṁśaka *and* Saddharmapuṇḍarīka besides others. The Mahāvastu which is the *Vinaya* of the Lōkōttaravādins[207] might have also been produced in these vihāras. It is noted that the Lōkōttaravādins were identical with the Caityakas,[208] the later term being ritualistic while the former philosophical. There is a strong tradition that Ācārya Nāgārjuna recovered the *Prajñā Pāramitā, Avataṁśaka,*[209] *and Saddharma puṇḍarīka* from Nāgaloka. The Nāgas were one of the tribes that have become part of the Āndhra race and Nāgaloka mentioned in the literature is identical with the mouths of the river Kṛṣṇa.[210] The tradition makes it clear therefore that the Mahāyāna literature was produced and was preserved in some of the early viharas of the Kṛṣṇā valley such as Bhaṭṭiprolu and Dhānyakaṭaka.

The *Gaṇḍavyūha,* another Mahāyāna Text of about the 3rd century A.D.,[211] contains an account of Bodhisattva Mañjuśrī. It says that Mañjuśrī who lived at Dhānyakaṭaka and converted a large number of Nāgas living around into Buddhism. Thus this account supports the view that it was a land of the Nāgas. Sudhāna, an enthusiastic Upasaka visited many places for Bodhisattva worship and finally reached Dhānyakaṭaka, where he met Mañjūśrī and learned from him *Sāmantabhadra Bodhicaryāvatāra.* The *Gaṇḍavyūha* thus makes it clear that Dhānyakaṭaka had been the centre of Bodhisattva practices over a long time.

According to the Ceylonese *Nikāya-saṅgraha,* the Andhakas produced the *Ratnakūṭa* literature.[212]

There is a strong tradition[213] recorded in the Tibetan texts that the śaila schools had a *Prajñapāramitā* in Prakrit. The Tummalagudem record proves that the Āndhra Buddhists were familiar with the system of six *Pāramitās.* The record describes the Buddha as *Ṣaḍabhijña,* one who has achieved the six perfections.

Edward Conze[214] and E.Lamote[215] are of the opinion that the two monasteries of the Mahāsaṅghikas, the Pūrvasaila and Aparaśaila on the Kṛṣṇa river had a *Prajñā pāramitā* in Prakrit. Further they say that they speak of Dharmadhātu in the same sense as the Prajñāpāramitā. The doctrines that Kathāvāttu attribute to the Andhakas are quite akin to the Mahāyāna doctrines and therefore they may well have developed them.

A passage in the Pāramitas[216] says that the Mahāyāna teachings will originate in the South migrate to the Eastern country and prosper in the north. It is clear that Mahāyāna originated in the Kṛṣṇā valley, migrated to Orissa and prospered at Nālanda.

Because of such over-whelming evidence, both epigraphical and literary, Bhikṣhu Sangharakshita says[217]: "Geographically, the Aṣṭāśāhaṣrika probably came from a spot near Amarāvatī and Nāgārjunakoṇḍa in the Āndhra country Aṣṭasāhaṣrika deals with the doctrine of emptiness ----".

Many scholars like Nalinaksha Dutt are of the same opinion.

It seems therefore reasonable to conclude that Mahāyānism had its origin in Āndhradēśa. It gradually developed from the principles and practices of the Caityaka-Mahāsaṅghika schools and became popular through the efforts of Ācārya Nāgārjuna and Āryadēva.

REFERENCES

1. E.J. Thomas, *The History of Buddhist Thought,* (London , 1963), p. 178
2. De La Valle poussin, *Encyclopaedia of Religion* and Ethics, Vol.VIII (under Mahāyānism).
3. A.B.Keith *Buddhist philosophy in India and Ceylon,* (Oxford, 1923), pp. 216-217.
4. *Ibid.*
5. M.Winternitz, *Some problems of Indian Literature,* (Calcutta, 1925) p. 63
6. Grierson, *"Bhakti Marga",* E.R.E., Vol.II, pp. 539-551.
7. Radhakumud Mukharjee, *Age of Imperial Unity,* (Ed.) Majumdar and Pusalker (Bombay, 1968), p. 97.
8. V.A. Smith (Ed,) *Cambridge Indian History,* p. 518
9. H.Kern, *Manual of Indian Buddhism,* (Delhi, 1974), p. 122.
10. J.Ph.Vogel, *Buddhist Art in India, Ceylon and Java,* (Delhi, 1977), (Indian Edition), pp. 21-22.
11. Foucher, *The beginnings of Buddhist Art and other essays in Indian and Central Asian Archaeology,* (Tr.) by L.A.Thomas and F.W.Thomas, (Delhi, 1972). p. 130.
12. Benjamen Rowland, *The Evolution of the Buddha Image.* (Newyork, 1976), p. 6.
13 Santa Ratnayaka, *The Boddhisattva Ideal of Theravada,* "the Journal of International Association of Buddhist Studies," (1985), Vol.VIII, No.2, pp. 85-110.
14. P.V.Bapat, (Ed.) 2500 *year of Buddhism,* (Delhi, 1956), p48.
15. *Ibid*
16. Hopkins, *The Religions of India,* R.V.IV, (Bostan, 1895), pp. 11-17.
17. E.J.Thomas, *History of Buddhist Thought,* p. 178.
18. A.B. Keith op. cit.
19. A.D.Hill *Bhagavadgītā,* (London, 1928), Introduction.
20. D.C.Sircar on Bhagavadgītā, *History and Culture of Indian people,* Vol.II, pp. 431-451.
21. H.Jacobi, E.R.E., Vol.VII, p. 195.
22. S.R.Goyal, *A.Religious History of Ancient India,* (Meerut, 1984), Vol.I, p. 360.
23. A.D.Hill op. cit., pp. 188-276.

24. Garbe, Di e *Bhagavatgītā,* quoted by R.C. pandeya in *Buddhist Studies in India,* p. 64.
25. Webers, *History of Indian Literature,* (Oriental Series, London, 1914), p. 238.
26. K.T.Telang, *Sacred Books of the East,* Vol.III, (Oxford, 1908)p. 21.
27. S.Radhakrishnan, (E.) *The Bhagavadgītā,* 6th Impression, (London, 1960), p. 14.
28. R.C. Pandeya, (Ed.) *Buddhist Studies in India,* (Delhi, 1975), pp. 44-60.
29. E.Hultzch, *Corpus Inscriptionum Indicarum,* Vol. I, Inscriptions of Āsoka, (Delhi, 1969), pp. XLix, Liv.
30. A.B.Keith, op. cit, p. 217.
31. Hardayal, *The Bodhisattva Doctrine in Buddhist Sanskrit Literature,* (Delhi, 1978), p. 32.
32. V.Trenckner and R.Chalmers (Ed.), *Majjimanikaya,* Vol.II, (London, 1888-99), pp. 176-210.
33. *Dhammapada,* (P.T.S., London, 1906-15), *Sukha Saddha Patitthita,* (Dhammapada, 333).
34. Hardayal, op. cit, p. 32.
35. G.C.Pande, *Studies in the Origins of Buddhism,* (Delhi, 1974), pp. 255-256.
36. Whitehead, *Village Gods of South India,* (Oxford, 1921), passim.
37. C.V.Narayana Aiyar, *Saivism in South India,* pp. 11-12.
38. H.Jacobi, *Jainism,* E.R.E. Vol.VII, p. 465.
39. A.L.Basham, *History and Doctrine of the Ajivikas - A Vanished Indian Religion,* (London, 1951) p. 284.
40. N.Dutt, *The Age of Imperial Unity,* (Bombay, 1968), p. 388.
41. Niharanjan Roy, *Maurya and post Maurya Art,* , (New Delhi, 1975), p. 65,
42. Ananda K.Coomaraswami, *The Origin of the Buddha Image,* (New Delhi), 1980), p. 17 and p. 18, fig.2.
43. R.G.Bhandarkar, *Vaiṣnavism, Saivism and Minor Religious* systems, *(poona,* 1928*),* p. 111.
44. Kautilay's *Arthaśāstra,* Quoted by B.P. Sinha, V, 2, XIII, 1, 2,"Significance of Religious data in kautilya's *Arthaśāstra, proceedings of Indian History Congress,* (Gauhati, 1954)
45. E.J.Thomas, *The History of Buddhist Thought,* pp. 169-170.
46. Kimura R., Mahāyāna and Hinayana Works known to Nāgārjuna, *Indian Historical Quarterly-III,* , pp. 412-417.

47. Winternitz, *Studies in the History of Indian Literature,* (Delhi, 1977), p 201 ff.
48. Johnston (Tr.) *Āsvaghosa's Buddha Carita,* Introduction.
49. Sahu, *Budhism in Orissa* (Utkal University, 1958) Passim.
50. N.Dutt, *Aspects of Mahāyāna and its relation to Hinayana,* (London, 1930), p. 43,
51. *Ibid.*
52. S. Dutt, *Buddhist Monks and Monasteries of India,* (London, 1967), page.136.
53. N.Dutt, op. cit, p. 40.
54. S.Z.Aung and Rhys Davids, *Points of Controversy,* (Oxford University press 1960), passim.
55. N.Dutt, I.H.Q. VII, p. 639.
56. N.Dutt, op. cit, p. 43.
57. Shaman Hwei, *Life of Yuan Chwang,* translated by samuel Beal, 2nd Edition (Delhi, 1973).
58. *Suttanipata,* Verse 1019. S.B.E. Vol. X.
59. P.S.Sastry, *"Rise and Growth of Buddhism in Āndhra,"* I.H.Q.XXXI, p. 68.
60. Rhys Davids and S.Z.Aung, *The points of Controversy,* passim.
61. D.C. Sircar, *Fragmentary pillar inscription from Amaravati, Epigraphia Indica* XXXV, p. 40 ff.
62. Ghosh and Sarkar*"Beginning of Sculptural Art in South East India - A.Stele from Amaravati"* *Ancient India,* (1967), p. 165.
63. D.C.Sircar, op. cit.
64. *Epigraphia Indica,* Vol. XXXV, p. 40. ff.
65 *Studies in Indian Epigraphy-I,* (1974), p. 60 ff.
66. I.K. Sarma, *Journal of the Epigraphical Society of India,* Vol. IX (1982), pp. 24-25.
67. *Ibid.*
68. T.N. Ramachandran. *Memoirs of Archaeological Survey of India* No.71 (Nāgārjunakonda, 1938), p. 1.
69. B.S.L.Hanumantha Rao, *Religion in Āndhra,* , (Guntur, 1973), p. 17.
70. N.Venkataramanayya, *Śatavahanna Commemoration Volume* (Guntur, 1946), presidential address.
71. C. Sivarāma Murthy, *Amaravati Sculptures in Madras Government Museum* (Madras, 1977), pls.Xliv, xlv, lxi, iv, xxxvi.xlv.

72. R.K.Mookerji, *Āsoka,* (Delhi, 1972), pp. 260-261.
73. *Ibid.*
74. Buhler--*Introduction to Āpastamba Sutras* - Sacred Book of the East, II, p. XLIII.
75. P.V. Kane, *History of Dharmaśāstra,* (Poona, 1930-58) 1, 1, p. 56.
76. Mc. Grindle, *Ancient India* (Megasthanes and Arrian) pp. 137-47.
77. *Arthaśāstra,* VII of Chatterjee, *Socio Economic Conditions in Early Āndhra.*, 200 B.C. to 300 A.D. (1976).
78. H.Sircar, Proceedings of the Āndhra Pradesh History Congress, Presidential Address, (Guntur, 1986). pp. 14-16.
79. Guru Raja Rao, *Megalithic Culture in South India.* (passim).
80. H.Sircar, op. cit, pp. 4-6, 14-16.
81. Mc. Crindle, *The Ancient Geography of India,* (Delhi, 1975), p. 457.
82. *Suttanipata.* Verses 1011-13.
83. K.A.Nilakanta Sastri (Ed.) *Age of the Nandas and Mauryas* (Delhi, 1967), p. 272.
84. I.Kartikeya Sarma, *"Guṇṭupalli", Journal of the Epigraphical Society of India,* Vol.V, p. 51.
85. *Epigraphia Andhrica,* Vol.II. p. 112.
86. I.Kartikey Sarma, *Coinage of the Śatavahana Empire,* (Delhi, 1980), p. 68
87. B.S.L.Hanumantha Rao, *"Traces of Roman Contact at Chebrolu", Āndhra Pradesh Journal,* 1964 - June
88. M.A.S.I., No. 54, p. 17.
89. Niharanjan Roy, Op. cit, p. 197.
90. White Head, *Village Gods of South India,* (passim).
91. R.P.Chanda *"Some Unpublished Amaravati Inscriptions". Epigraphia Indica, Vol.XV, pp.* 258-275.
92. *B.S.L.Hanumantha Rao, Religion in Āndhra, pp.* 18-19.
93. *Ananda K.Coomaraswami, Yakshas, Vol.I, pp.* 17-24.
94. B.S.L.Hanumantharao, op. cit.
95. Ananda K.Coomaraswami, op. cit.
96. Guru Raja Rao, op. cit (passim).
97. *Burgess, Buddhist Stupas of Amaravati and Jaggayyapeta, (London,* 1887*)* p. 23.
98. Vaddlamanu Excavations and Explorations in Krishna Valley *(Birla Archaeological and Cultural Research Institute) (Hyderabad), page.*4.

99. Burgess, op. cit p. 23, pl.xlv, 3.
100. M.A.S.I., No.54, p. 17.
101. C.Śivarāmamurthy, op. cit, p. 20.
102. As early as the 3rd Century A.D. at Nāgārjunakoṇḍa, an image of Mother Goddess was installed by a lady for the longevity of her husband and her son. H.K.Narasimha Swamy, E.I., Vol. XXIX, p. 137.
103. *D.C.Sircar on "Bhagavadgītā" in Age of Imperial Unity*, p. 440.ff
104. P.V.Kane, *History of Dharma Śastra,* (Poona, 1930-58) p. 57.
105. *Nanaghat Inscription of Nāganika, Archaeological Survey of Western India,* Vol.V, p. 60 ff. 39
106. B.S.L.Hanumantha Rao, *Religion in Āndhra,* Appendix-I, pp. 321-323.
107. E.I.Volume VIII, Nasik Inscriptions, No.22.
108. E.I. Volume 10, (Luders List) Inscription, no. 1024.
108-a. E.I. Volume X LL No. 1001.
109. *Ibid* 1007.
110. *Ibid* 1060.
111. *Ibid*, 1054.
112. *Ibid*, 1072.
113. Sircar, op. cit, pp 440-441.
114. Sir Charles Eliot, *Hinduism and Buddhism* (London, 1957), Volume I, p. 41.
115. Megasthanes sees the Greek Gods, Dionysus and Herakles in the Indian Gods of Śiva and Kṛṣṇa Sir Charles Eliot, *Hinduism and Buddhism*, Vol.II, p. 138.
116. Radhakumud Mukharji, Sungas, *Age of Imperial Unity*, p. 98.
117. Alchin, *Birth of Indian Civilization,* Trider & alchin Series (1968), p. 317.
118. R.G.Bandarkar, op. cit, p. 111.
119. B.L.Rice, *Epigraphia Carnatica,* Vol.VII, p. 14.
120. Cf. C.Śivarāmamurty, *Indian sculptures*, p. 47, fig.6.
121. R.G.Bandarkar, op. cit, p. 104.
122. Gatha Saptāsati-I, 35, (Bombay, 1869).
123. E.I. Vol.VIII, Nasik Ins. No.19, p. 60 ff.
124. B.Jinananda, "Four Buddhist Councils", *2500 Years of Buddhism,* (ed.) P.V.Bapat, pp. 41-44.
125. dela Valli poussin, op. cit, J.R.A.S. 1910, pp. 413-23.

126. N.Dutt, *The Age of Imperial Unity*, p. 390.
127. E.I., Vol.XX pp. 17-20.
128. *Epigraphia Andhrica,* Vol.II, p. 10.
129. R. Subrahmaniam, *Salihuṇdam*, pp. 55, No. 41 & pp. 85, No.22.
130. N.Dutt, "Notes on Nāgārjunakoṇda Inscriptions, I.H.Q.Vol.VII, p. 733.
131. Burgess, op. cit, p. 105.
132. E.I., Vol.XX, p. 19.
133. The Abhidhamma of the Theravadins was in seven parts. The only known Abhidhamma in five parts is that of the Dharmaguptikas, N.Dutt, op. cit.
134. Burgess, op. cit, p. 24.
135. E.I. Vol.X, No.1248.
136. C.Śivarāma Murthy, *Amaravati Sculptures in Madras Government Museum,* p. 278.
137. E.I. Vol.X, *Luders List,* no. 1223, F.1263.
138. *Ibid*, 1250.
139. Burgess, *Notes on Amaravati Stupa,* (Madras, 1882), p. 4.
140. *Ibid*, p. 44.
141. Alexander Rea, *A.R.A.S.I.* (1910-11), p. 75, pl.VL III, No.20.
142. E.I., Vol. XXIV, pp. 256-258, The Dharanikota pillar inscription says that the Mahācaitya was in the possession of the Pūrvaśailas
143. E.J.Thomas, op. cit, Appendix II p. 287.
144. Mrs. Rhys Davids, *Points of Controversy,* op. cit, p Xliii, ff.
145. B.C.Law (Tr.), *Kathāvattu-Aṭṭhakatha* - (P.T.S.), (London, 1940), pp. 54-55.
146. H.Sircar, *Ancient India* No.16, p. 81.
147. E.J.Thomas, op. cit, p. 173.
148. P.V.Bapat, op. cit, p. 118.
149. *Ibid*.
150. *J.R.A.S.*, 1910, pp. 414-423.
151. E.Lamotte, "Buddhist Controversy over the five propositions, *I.H.Q.*, Vol. 32, (1985), p. 148-62.
152. E.I., Vol.XXXV, pp. 11-13.
153. T.R.V.Murthy, op. cit, p.•6.
154. P.V.Bapat (ed.) op. cit. p. 120.
155. Mrs. Rhys Davids, op. cit, p. XI.3.

156. Burgess. *Buddhist Stupas of Amaravati and Jaggayyapeta* Pls.XXII, I:L2; xxvi.
157. *Kathāvatthu,* XVII, 6, 10: XVIII, 1.
158. Oldenberg, *Dīpavaṁsa,* xxii (London, 1978), p. 45.
159. S.N.Dube, *Cross Currents in Early Buddhism,* (New Delhi, 1980), p. 75.
160. *Kathāvatthu,* XXIII, 1, *Ekadhippayena methuno,* dhammo patisevitabho ti..
161. S.N.Dube, op. cit, p. 208.
162. *Sukumara Dutt, Buddhist Monks and Monasteries of India. (London,* 1967*),* p. 136.
163. *Ibid.*
164. E.I., Vol.X, No.1235, 1240, 1271, 1285 etc.
165. *Buhler,* "A note on the word Siddham used in the Inscriptions", *I.A., X,* p. 273.
166. Burgess, B.S.A.J., p. 72.
167. *Ibid,*
168. E.I., Vol.XX, pp. 15-16.
169. E.I., Vol.XX, Apsidal Temple Inscription No.F.
170. *Ibid*, p. 22.
171. E.I., Vol.XX, pp. 23-24.
172. E.I. Vol.XXXVI, p. 274.
173. Burgess, *Notes on Amaravati Stupa.* p. 54.
174. *Epigraphia Āndhrika*, Vol.II, pp. 9-11.
175. E.J.Thomas, *History of Buddhist Thought,* p. 149.
176. Hardayal, *The Bodhisattva Doctrine in Buddhist Sanskrit Literature,* (Delhi, 1978), pp. 20-21.
177. The *Aveṇika Dharmas* otherwise termed Buddha Dharmas or qualities of a Buddha. These are: (1) The seeing of all things past, (2) Of all things future, (3) of all things present, (4) Propriety of actions of the body, (5) of speach, (6) of thought, (7) firmness of intention, (8) of memory, (9) of Samādhi, (10) of energy, (11) of emancipation, (12) of wisdom, (13) freedom from ficklencss of wantonness, (14) from noisiness, (15) from confusedness, (16) from hastiness, (17) from heedlessness, (18) from inconsiderateness, H.Kern, *Manual of Indian Buddhism,* (Delhi, 1972) p. 63.
178. *Hardayal, op. cit,* p. 20.
179. *Select Inscriptions,* , Vol.I, p. 215 ff.

180. *E.I., Vol.XX, C3, C4, B2, B4.*
181. *E.R.E., Vol.IV* pp. 739-53.
182. P.R.Ramachandra Rao, *The Art of Nāgārjunakoṇḍa,* (Madras, 1956), pl.XXXI, p. 96.
183. Aiyappan and P.R. Srinivasan (ed.) *Story of Buddhism with Special Reference to South India.* pp. 65-67.
184. *Ibid.*
185. Burgess, *Buddhist Stupas of Amaravati and Jaggayyapeta, pl.XII, XL,* 2, *pl.XXI & C. Śivarāma Murthy, op. cit, pl.Xv.*
186. *Select Inscriptions,* Vol.I, p. 215, ff.
187. C. Śivarāma Murty, *Amaravati Sculptures,* in the Madras government Museum op. cit, plate 91.
188. *Select Inscriptions,* Vol.I, p 215 ff.
189. *Burgess, Pl.III, VI,* p. 98.
190. *Longhurst, M.A.S.I.,* No.71, pl.XIXI, a.
191. R.Subrahmanyam, *Śalihuṇḍam* (Hyderabad, 1960), p. 132.
192. N.Dutt, *Buddhist sects in India* (Delhi, 1978), p. 83.
193. *M.A.S.I., No,* 71, *pl.XIV A&B.*
194. *E.I., Vol. XXXV,* pp. 12-13.
195. Burgess, *B.S.A.J.,* p. 112.
196. C.Śivarāma Murthy, op. cit, No.60 and Burgess, *Notes on Amaravati Stupa.* p. 49.
197. *Ibid.*
198. *Journal of Indian History, XL III, pt.*3.
199. E.I., Vol. XXXVIII, p. 318.
200. E.I., Vol.XX, Detached pillar Inscription - H.
201. E.I., Vol.XX, p. 16, Ayakapillar Inscription C3.
202. E.I., Vol.XX, Nāgārjunakoṇda apsidal temple Inscription No.F.
203. E.I., Vol.XX, Nāgārjunakoṇḍa Inscription, No.H.
204. E.I., Vol.X, p. 247.
205. E.I., Vol.XXXV, pp. 11-13.
206. Burgess, op. cit, pp. 112-206.
207. *E.R.E., Vol.viii,* Dc La Valle poussin, *Mahāvastu,* p. 328.
208. P.V.Bapat, (Ed.) 2500 *Years of Buddhism,* p. 118.
209. Aiyappan and P.R. Srinivasan (Ed) *Story of Buddhism with Special Reference to South India,* p. 118.
210. K.A.N.Sastri, *Foreign Notices of South India,* (Madras, 1939), p. 97.

211. N.Dutt, I.H.Q., Vol.VII, p. 639.
212. K.Satchidananda Murthy, *Āndhra Contribution to Buddhist Thought* (Dr. S.Radhakrishnan Memorial Lecture) (Hyderabad, 1980), p. 12.
213. Edward Conze, *The Prajñā Pāramita Literature,* p. 9
214. Edward Conze, *The Perfection of Wisdom Śutras,* Sangharakshita (ed.) *Eternal Legacy, (London,* 1985*),* p. 134.
215. *B.S.L.Hanumantha Rao, Religon in Āndhra,* p. 100.
216. N. Dutt, *Aspects of Mahāyana and its relation to Hinayāna Buddhism,* p. 43.
217. Sangharakshita, *A Survey of Buddhism* (Bangalore, 1957) p. 321.
218. N. Dutt, op. cit, p. 43.

CHAPTER - III

MAHĀYĀNA PHILOSOPHERS OF ĀNDHRADĒŚA

Nalinaksha Dutt rightly observes : "It appears that the South may claim credit for being not only the birth place of Mahāyāna itself but also of the noted figures, who were instrumental in making Mahāyāna what it was in the 2nd and 3rd centuries A.D.[1] Dutt has in Mind Ācārya Nāgārjuna and Āryadeve only. But Āndhra was the home of many more Mahāyāna philosophers. In course of time Mahāyāna branched off into Madhyamika and Yogācara Schools.[2]

Whereas Nāgārjuna was the founder of the Madhyamika system, the founder of Yogācara was Maitreyanātha.[3] According to some scholars Maitreyanātha flourished some time between 270-350 A.D.[4] It is held by some that[5] Maitreyanātha was also a native of Āndhra and his native place was Potala or Paudanyapura, identified with modern Bodhan[6] in the Nizamabad district. But their arguements are not convincing. However two of the champions of Yogācara, Dignāga[7] and Dharmakīrti lived and worked in Āndhradēśa.[8]

Even the Mādhyamika school of Nāgārjuna came to be divided into Prāsaṅgika[9] and Svātantrika[10] schools expounded by Buddhapālita and Bhāvavivēka respectively, and both of them were natives of Āndhradēśa as will be seen in the following pages.

ĀCĀRYA NĀGĀRJUNA

Ācārya Nāgārjuna who had illuminated the Buddhist world with his intellectual eminence, is considered as one of the greatest philosophers, the world has ever produced. Devout Buddhists of China, Japan, Tibet and Bhutan consider him to be the Second Buddha who once again set in motion the wheel of Dharma. Zenryu Tsukamoto says that he was the first and the greatest organiser of Mahāyāna doctrine.[11] According to Sir Charles Eliot : Nāgārjuna represents a movement and a school as much as a personality".[12] Thomas Watters calls him "The wonder and mystery of later Buddhism".[13] K.R. Subramanian describes him as "The Aristotle of Buddhist lore, the Christ of Mādhyamika and St. Paul of Mahāyāna, a magical name baffling the most brainy in sheer intellectual power and moral force".[14]

NATIVITY:- The history of such a great luminary is shrouded in obscurity. Every aspect of his life is a subject of controversy. It is but natural that the native place of such a great man is likely to be a matter of dispute. The general consensus among scholars is that he was born in a Brāhmin family in Dakshināpatha, which is identified by some with Vidarbha.[15] But some say that Nāgārjuna was born in a place to the South of Vidarbha.[16] The Chinese version of *Mahā Mēgha Sūtra* says that in the time of King Śātavāhana a great monk Nāgarāja was born in a village Kusumamāla or Sumanamāla near the river Supaya in the kingdom of Surāṣṭra in South India.[17] It appears that there is much confusion in this work. Neither Surāṣṭra is in South India nor the Śātavāhanas held sway over Surāṣṭra during this period.

The *Lankavatāra Śūtra* says "The great monk Nāgahvaya was born in Vēdali in South India, put an end to the extreme views on being and non-being".[18] Among the Brāhmins of Āndhra there are some with Vedula as their family name. It is a known fact that most of the family names in Āndhra are place names.[19]

According to a tradition recorded in the *Blue Annals*, Nāgārjuna was born at a place east of Śrīparvata and west of Śrīsthana.[20] The latter word was a shortened form of Śrī Dhānyakaṭaka.[21] If the accounts of *Lankavatāra Sūtra* and *Blue Annals* are read together, we come to the conclusion that Nāgārjuna was born at Vēdali which may be located in the region of Palnad, though it cannot be identified at present. There is every possibility of Vedali being misunderstood as Vidarbha.

DATE

Different accounts give Nāgārjuna different dates. The *Mañjuśrī Mūlakalpa* says that 400 years after the Buddha's *Parinirvāna* a monk called Nāgahvaya appeared, and lived for 600 years.[22] The *Laṅkāvatāra* gives the same date for the birth of Nāgārjuna as 400 years after *Parinirvāṇa,*[23] According to these accounts the date of Nāgārjuna's birth is 176 B.C.

The *Mahāmaya Sūtra* says that 700 years after *Mahāparinirvāṇa* the monk Nāgārjuna appeared.[24] Thus it means 224 A.D. These dates are not acceptable because the former is too early and the latter too late for the birth of Nāgārjuna. Literary accounts about Nāgārjuna's date are thus confusing and therefore not entirely dependable. After discussing several hypothesis, Winternitz places Nāgārjuna in the later half of the 2nd century A.D.[25], which is accepted by most scholars.[26]

The Tibetan tradition which says that Nāgārjuna lived for 600 years[27] is very interesting and is connected with the problem of the number of Nāgārjunas in the history of Buddhism. There is every reason to believe that there were more than one Nāgārjuna. We have seen that there is consensus that Ācarya Nāgārjuna, the founder of Mādhyamaka lived around 200 A.D. An inscription[28] from Jaggayyapeta speaks about Bhadanta Nāgārjuna and his disciple Jayaprabha who was a teacher of Chandraprabha. In his recent book on Nāgārjuna, K. Satchidananda Murtly holds the view that there was only one Nāgārjuna, the Mādhyamika philosopher, who is identical with Bhadanta Nāgārjuna of Jaggayyapeta record and places him around 200 A.D[29] But on the grounds of paleography the record is assigned to the middle of the 6th C.A.D.[30] Therefore Bhadanta Nāgārjuna of the above record cannot be held identical with Ācarya Nāgārjuna. From this record it is evident that about the 5th century A.D. there was another Nāgārjuna. The Tibetan tradition might have held the two, namely Ācarya Nāgārjuna and Bhadanta Nāgārjuna identical and gave Ācarya Nāgārjuna a long life of 600 years.[31].

CONTEMPORAṆEITY WITH KANISHKA

Some historians believe that Kanishka and Nāgārjuna, were contemporaries[32] but many others doubt it.[33] In the heirarchy of Buddhist patriarchs,[34] Nāgārjuna is the fifteenth whereas Āsvaghosa, the contemporary of Kanishka is the thirteenth. Therefore there is atleast a gap of one generation between Kanishka and Nāgārjuna. In the Fourth Buddhist Council, held in the time of Kanishka, Mahāyāna Buddhism was not represented.[35] It was Nāgārjuna who systematised and popularised Mahāyānism.

According to Kalhana's *Rājatarangiṇi*, [36] the Bodhisattva Nāgārjuna was "The only lord of the land" in Kashmir at the period of the kings Huska, Juska and Kanishka. The last king is evidently Kanishka[37] II.

CONTEMPORANEITY WITH THE ŚATAVAHANAS

The general concensus of opinion among scholars is that Ācārya lived during the Śatavāhana period. But different scholars make him the contemporary of Hala[38] the *Kavivatsala* and Gautamiputra, [39] the Ekabrahmaṇa and Gautamiputra Srī Yajña.[40] Yuan-chwang calls the patron of Nāgārjuna as Yen-ching[41] and that he ruled over a vast empire including even Central India. Even Bāṇabhāṭta says that the patron of Nāgārjuna was the lord of the three oceans.[42] This account agrees well with the history of Śrī Yajña.[43] The above date 200 A.D. for Nāgārjuna makes it impossible that Nāgārjuna was a contemporary of the first two kings, Hala[44] and Gautamīputra Śatakarṇi.[45] Śrī Yajña flourished in the last quarter of the 2nd century A.D.[46] and therefore it may be concluded that he was the patron of Ācārya Nāgārjuna.

EDUCATION

The biography of Nāgārjuna was translated into the Chinese by Kumārajīva circa 400 A.D.[47] But his account of the early life is overlaid with incredible legendary material. However, it appears that he had studied thoroughly the Brāhmanical canonical literature before he accepted Buddhism. Then he mastered the three *Piṭakas* in a short time. It is said that Nāgārjuna was not satisfied with the interpretations given by his teachers on the teachings of the Buddha, which according to him must be comprehensive.[48] He therefore announced that he had no master and made up his mind to rewrite the treatises on *dharma* basing on a consistent logically argued philosophy.[49]

RECOVERY OF VAIPULYA SŪTRAS

At this stage, Nāgārjuna is said to have met Mahānāga of Nāgalōka, and the latter presented to Nāgārjuna the *Vaipulyasūtras.*[50] All the accounts of his life speak that he had obtained the *Prajñāpāramitā Sūtras* from a Nāga king. Kumārajīva calls the Nāga chief as Mahānāga who led Nāgārjuna to the sea and opened for him the "Treasury of the seven jewels".[51] The Nāgaloka of these accounts is identified with the region around the mouths of the river Kṛṣṇā.[52]

SETTLEMENT AT ŚRĪPARVATA

According to the tradition recorded in the Tibetan work, at Śrīparvata[53] Śrī Yajña Śātakarṇi built for Nāgārjuna a Mahācaitya and a Mahāvihāra. The association of the Śatavāhanas with Śrīparvata is attested by the inscription of Vijayaśātakarṇi dated in his 6th regnal year.[54] It may be taken as an additional support to the historicity of the Tibetan tradition, that Nāgārjuna had his Mahācaitya and Mahāvihāra at Śrīparvata where he collected a huge library of Mahāyāna texts. It is probable that the place was selected by Nāgārjuna himself for his settlement as it was by the side of a provincial head-quarters[55] and besides Setagiri, [56] which was already a place of religious significance, frequently visited by pious pilgrims. Nāgārjuna made Śrīparvata the centre of his religious and philosophical activities.

Nāgārjuna is the greatest dialectician the world has ever seen. Still he had a realistic eye to understand the condition and requirements of Buddhism in his time. He appears to have examined the existing literature and systematised the Buddhist philosophy and gave it a set of religious practices which breathed a new life into Buddhism, and made it popular in the face of virulent Brāhmanical revival.[58]

The role of Nāgārjuna in the elaboration of this literature is defined by Kern[59] thus : "Nāgārjuna may have been one of the most talented and influential leaders of the movement rather than its originator. Again he says that the figure of Nāgārjuna, so prominent in the history of the rise of Mahāyāna shows a double character. It is on one side the name of an influential person, the first eminent leader of a school imbued with Hinduism and the methods of Indian scholastic philosophy. On the other hand Nāgārjuna is simply the comprehensive name of the activity of Mahāyānism in the first phase of its onward course. The intellectual eminence of Nāgārjuna and the large number of dialectical and philosophical works attributed to him made some scholars to doubt even the historicity of Nāgārjuna.[60]

HIS DEATH

There is a tradition that Ācarya Nāgārjuna was a devotee of Amitābha of whom he had a vision at Dhānyakaṭaka and that he died with his face turned towards *Sukhāvati.*[61] On the other hand the *Kathāsaritsāgara* gives an interesting account about the death of Nāgārjuna.[62] According to it, Nāgārjuna discovered the elixir of life and by administering it he prolonged the life of his patron king. The queen and the crown prince grew tired of the long life of the king, and having known the secret of it, the prince went to the Vihara of Nāgārjuna and asked for his life. Nāgārjuna readily offered his own head to the prince. This account has been repeated by Yuan Chwang[63] also. It is not impossible to reconcile the two accounts.

HIS WORKS

As many as 24 works have been attributed to Nāgārjuna, but it is difficult to know exactly how many of them are authentic.[64] There is some similarity in the contents of the works attributed to him and they exhibit the essential features of Nāgārjuna's philosophy. Nāgārjuna is said to have been the originator of a new system in Sanskrit literature known as *Kārika*[65] which is the *śloka* and *vyākhyāna* by the same author. He composed the Mūlamādhyamika in that style and the *vyākhyāna* (commentary) to it is called *Akuthobhayā.*[66]

Most of Nāgārjuna's works are found only in the Tibetan and Chinese languages. Among them, the most important works are:

(1) *Prajñā Pāramitā śāstra ṭīkā*

(2) *Mūla Mādhyamika Kārikā - and commentary Akutobhaya*

(3) *Vigrahavyāvartani*

(4) *Daśabhūmi Vibhāṣa śāstra*

(5) *Ratnāvali*

(6) *Suhṛllekha*

(7) *Dvādasa Nikāya śāstra*

(8) *Pratītya samutpāda Hṛdaya*

(9) *Śūnyata-saptati*

(10) *Vaidalya Sūtra and prakaraṇa*

(11) *Sutra Samuccaya*

Prajñā-Pāramita.

Max Muller says that this great B'ıddhist philosopher trod the path of *prajñā-pāramitā* and wrote even the vyākhyāna in order to expound the basic teachings of the *Prajñā-Pāramitā śāstra.*[67] On the basis of the śastra, Nāgārjuna propounded the Madhyamika system which is the systematised form of the *Śūnyatā* doctrine. Its metaphysical thought and religious ideal are all present therein. With the *Prajñā-Pāramitā* literature an entirely revolutionary phase of Buddhism begins.[68] A severe type of absolutism established by the dialectic by the negation *Śūnyata*) of all empirical notions and speculative theories, replaces the pluralism and dogmatism of the earlier Buddhism.[69] In fact the *Prajñaparamitā śutras* are not innovations. They are only expositions of the deeper and profound teachings of the Buddha. The word *Prajñā-pāramitā* is generally translated as "perfect wisdom".[70] The word *pāramitā* that is 'gone beyond' suggests that it would be better to translate, *prajñā Pāramita* as transcendent wisdom or transcendent insight. The *Prajñā-pāramitā* is both philosophy and religion. The Principal theme of the *Prajña Pāramitā* literature is the doctrine of *Śūnyatā. Prajñā* or transcendent insight consists in ceasing to indulge in thought constructions. So, *Prajñā* becomes synonymous with *Śūnyatā,* which is the final truth. In all countries where Mahāyāna is a living religion, the following *prajñāpāramita mantra* is generally recited: "*Gate Gate, Pāramgate, Pārasaṅgate, Bodhi Svāhā* i.e., "O wisdom which has gone beyond the beyond, to thee Homage".[72]

VIGRAHA VYĀVARTANI

This work gives a clear insight into the Madhyamika

dialectics, Nāgārjuna composed it in reply to certain criticisms, levelled against his *Madhyamakakārika by Vatsyāyana* T.R.V. Murty observes that *Vigraha Vyāvartani* is the refutation of possible objections that may be raised against the negative method of *Śūnyatā* dialectic.

DAŚABHŪMI VIBHĀSĀ ŚĀSTRA

It tells that true existence *(svabhāva)* is non existence *(abhāva).*[74] Another philosophical treatise of Nāgārjuna is the *Mahāyāna Viṁśaka.*[75] Here Nāgārjuna taught that" there is neither *samsara* nor *nirvāṇa* and that every thing is mere illusion and dream".[76]

RATNĀVAḶĪ

The Ratnāvaḷī was written as a piece of advice to a king, to whom probably the *Suhrillekha* was also addressed. The work is not completely discovered. only four chapters, 1, 2, 4, and 5 have been found in the Tibetan. The first three have been discovered, translated and published by the Italian scholar Tucci[77] and the 5th chapter by the German scholar Prof. Michael Hahn.[78] In it Nāgārjuna criticises false doctrines, establishes the superiority of Mahāyāna, [79] but emphasises the importance of tolerance.[80] He advises the king to abstain from drink and listen to wise counsels and on matters of administration, he also suggests to abolish the capital punishment. It reveals that Nāgārjuna conceives a state just on the lines of a welfare state.[81]

SUHṚLLEKHA

The title means Letter to a Friend, who was Nāgārjuna's patron king. It is available only in the Tibetan and now translated into English. He advises the king on the basic principles of the Buddhist religion. It is in one hundred and twenty three verses.[82] Several verses of the work resemble those of Pāli Dhammapada. The Chinese pilgrim, I-tsing praises this work of Nāgārjuna very highly and reports that in his days he found children committing it to memory and adults making a life long study of it.[83]

DVĀDAŚA NIKĀYA ŚĀSTRA

In this Nāgārjuna expounds the greatness of Mahāyāna. It is superior to Hīnayāna because it helps people to reach the ideal of Buddhahood. It is ridden by Buddhas and great men, Bodhisattvas like Avalokiteśwara, Mañjuśrī and Maitreya[84] etc. It can eliminate the sufferings of sentient beings and give great benefits. It leads to the ultimate truth.[85]

HIS PHILOSOPHY

Nāgārjuna ushered a revolution in Buddhist philosophy, through his concept of Sūnyatā. He made use of the term Madhyamā pratipad, the middle path, used by Buddha to characterise his teachings and called his philosophy Madhyamaka (Madhyamaiva Madhyamakaṁ).

Nāgārjuna pondered deeply over the silence of Buddha on certain important questions, and came to the conclusion that the reason of Buddha's studied silence was that reality was transcendental to thought.

Nāgārjuna's Mādhyamika system declares that phenomera are neither positive or negative, but merely relative. His work begins with the famous eight negations, but it is here expressly stated that they mean the same as the doctrine of causality or dependent origination. No passing away and no origination, no destruction and no everlasting continuence, no unity and no multiplicity, no coming and no going. This may lead to an absurd situation. If everything is "empty" and there is neither origination nor passing away, then there can also be no four noble Truths and no rule of life based on the knowledge of these truths, no fruit of good and evil deeds, no Buddha doctrine (dharma) no monastic community and finally also no Buddha.[86] Thus the entire religion of the Buddha collapses into Nothingness. But Nāgārjuna replies: "The doctrine of the Buddha rests on two truths; one conventional truth (*samvṛti* or *laukika satya*) in which the deeper meaning remains hidden and the other is the highest (paramārtha) truth. He who does not know the distinction between these two truths, does not understand the profound substance of the Buddha doctrine. The highest truth can be understood only when based on the truth of every day life, and without the assistance of the highest truth, it is not possible to understand Nirvāṇa. "That which covers all round is samvṛti. Samvṛti is (ajñāna) which covers the real nature of all things." Phenomena is characterised as Samvṛti because they throw a veil over reality. At the same time they serve as a pointer to reality as their ground. Samvṛti Satya is vyavahārika satya (pragmatic or empirical reality). Paramārtha satya is absolute reality. Nāgārjuna expressly mentions the importance of vyavahāra or empirical reality in attaining paramārtha or absolute reality. Nāgārjuna says that "Without a recourse to pragmatic reality the absolute cannot be taught. Without knowing absolute truth Nirvāṇa cannot be attained."[87]

It is the transcendental truth which eradicates duality. It is emptiness (śūnyatā), suchness (Tathata) and the essence of reality (dharmadhātu, dharmata) it is seeing the nature of things as they are (yathābhūthaṁ), realising all things to be empty in their nature. Prajñā is to see things in their true mental relations and in relation to the ground of their appearance, removing the veil of multiplicity which covers them.

ĀRYADĒVA

Āryadēva was the principal disciple of Nāgārjuna and is considered as the second greatest Mādhyamika philosopher. The age of Nāgārjuna-Āryadēva was the heyday in the history of Āndhra Buddhism. Āryadēva is known by other names also such as Deva, Kāṇadeva, one eyed deva and Nīla Nētra "the blue eyed."[88]

NATIVITY

Mañjuśrī-Mūlatantra assigns Āryadēva to Saihnika pura and calls him a non-Āryan.[89] Buston following the lead of this Text puts him in Siṁhaḷa.[90] Some Tibetan chronicles observe that his father ruled over Sen-ga-glin, [91] while other sources says that he was the adopted son of the king of Siṁhaḷa. According to Chandrakīrti he was the crown prince of Siṁhaḷa[92] which S.W.Laden-la identified with Guntur District.[93]

According to Kumārajīva, Āryadēva was a Brāhmin of South India.[94] Yuan chwang speaks of Devapūṣa as Chishih-Tzu-kuo which may be a transliteration or a rendering of Siṁhadhara putrapura.[95] According to the story recorded in the Bṛhatkathā, Dīpakarṇi, the king of Śrīkakuḷam found a prince riding on the back of a lion (Siṁhadhara) and adopted him as his son.[96] The boy became Sātavāhana, Sāta being the name of the lion, and became the founder of the Sātavāhana dynasty.[97]

P.S.Sastri identifies Sen-ga-glin with Śrīkākuḷam near Machilīpaṭṇam[98] on the banks of the river Kṛṣṇā. According to the traditional account Śrīkākuḷam was the original home of the Sātavāhanas.[99] This eminently agrees with Yuan chwang's statement that Āryadēva was a native of Siṁhadharaputrapura which according to Bṛhatkathā was Śrīkākuḷam and this Śrīkākuḷam is in the north-east of Nāgārjunakoṇḍa. The identification again justifies Chandrakīrti's statement that Āryadēva came south-west to meet Nāgārjuna.

Gustava Charles Toussainst[101] takes this Sen-ga-glin to refer to a country not far from Udyān or Urgyan in the Dhānyakaṭaka area. Dr. Waddel equated it with the Siṁhapura of Yuan Chwang. All these point to Śrīkākuḷam as the native place of Āryadēva. As the town is on the banks of the Kṛṣṇā in the delta, there is every possibility of its being mistaken for an island. K.S.Murty states that there is no doubt that Āryadēva's main centre of activity was Āndhra.[103]

DATE

About the date of Āryadēva also there is much confusion. Kumārajīva places him between A.D. 163-263.[104] In the list of Buddhist patriarchs the name of Āryadēva is found immediately after that of Nāgārjuna[105] and tradition says that Āryadeva was the most important disciple of Nāgārjuna and succeeded him in the patriarchate. Both Yuan Chwang and I-tsing mention Āryadēva along with Aśvaghoṣa and Nāgārjuna as one of the great men who lived in ancient times.[106] Therefore the date of Kumārajīva appears to be reasonable.

The Chinese works give some interesting points about

the relationship between Nāgārjuna and Āryadēva. Āryadēva went to Nāgārjuna to discuss some of the points of the canon. To test the scholarship of Āryadēva, Nāgārjuna sent a bowl of water to Āryadēva in which the latter dropped a needle. Nāgārjuna explained it that the bowl of water represents his own knowledge and by throwing a needle in it Āryadēva replied that he had seen the bottom of it.[107] Nāgārjuna was impressed with the intelligence of Āryadeva and trained him as his successor.

HIS WORKS

Five treatises extant in Tibetan are attributed to Āryadeva. These are :(1) Catuḥśataka (2) Hastavāla-Prakaraṇa (3) Akṣaraśataka (4) Jñānasāra-samuccaya and (5) Cittaviśudhi prakaraṇa.[108]

SIGNIFICANCE OF HIS WORKS

The Catuḥśataka is the most famous of Āryadeva's works. Like the Madhyamakaśāstra it consists of 400 kārikās. It is one of the fundamental works of the Mādhyamika school. Deva defends Nāgārjuna's doctrines not only as against other Buddhist schools but also against Brahmanical systems, especially the Vaiśeṣikas. In it, Deva draws an emphatic distinction between the two kinds of knowledge.

Sing chao, in his preface to the Catuhśataka says "The Catuḥ Śataka is the ford and the road that provides access to the holy mind, the essential treatise that opens up the absolute truth".[109]

The method adopted by Āryadeva was different from that of Nāgārjuna. Āryadeva occasionally discusses the arguments of opponents, analyses them and taking note of the differences among them and then exposes their weaknesses. Āryadeva links the doctrine of emptiness with life and behaviour of a Bodhisattva and the doctrine of two fold truth-Samvṛtisatya and Paramārthasatya. In the first half of Catuḥ Śataka, Āryadeva expounds his Dharma and in the second he exposes the views of his opponents and demolishes them.[110] Here Āryadēva expresses his views on Yoga.

HASTAVĀLA PRAKARAṆA

The Hastavāla-prakaraṇa may be taken as another attempt by Āryadēva at summarising the doctrines in a few verses. Just as the "rope-snake" is unreal, the things of the world too, when closely scrutinised, are equally unreal.[111] The wise one should abandon attachment, just as one shakes off the fear of the unreal rope-snake'. At the end of the work, Āryadeva tries to bring out the distinction between laukika-satya and paramārtha-satya.

AKṢARA ŚATAKA

The Akṣaraśataka is the other important work of Āryadeva, It is lost in the original, but is preserved in the Chinese and Tibetan. There are doubts with regard to the genuineness of the work, Gokhale remarks: "As regards the short basic text, the Akṣara Śataka proper it is by no means improbable that Āryadēva was the author of it."[112] He adds that one might easily be tempted to suggest a chronological sequence among his works—Catuḥ-śataka, Śata Śāstra and Akṣara Śataka. The logical arguements started in Catuḥ-Śataka become more and more systematic and pointed in the Akṣara-Śataka. The arguements contain refutation of the views of the Sāmkhyas and Vaiśeṣikas, probably prominent in Āryadēva's times.

CITTAVIŚUDDHI PRAKARAṆA

It deals with "the purification of the mind". It is a didactic poem, containing among other things[113] arguments against the Brāhmanical ceremonial system. Only fragments of the work have come down to us.

HIS TEACHINGS

Āryadēva taught that everything in the phenomenal world is unreal and that one should reflect upon the true meaning of all things. There is neither murdered nor murderer and neither friend nor foe. If salvation could be attained by bathing in the Ganges, he says, a fisherman would attain salvation and more particularly the fish which live in the river day and night.[114] He prescribes different sets of rules to different people according to their mental capacity. He prescribes charity (dāna) to the people at a low level, marality (śīla) to those at the middle level and peace (śānti) to those at a higher level.[115] According to Āryadēva peace is obtained by realising the emptiness. He indicated a gradual process of Yoga, in the last stage of which śūnyatā is realised. He is said to have been fond of preaching the Andhakavinda suttānta.[116]

The Mādhyamika system owes much of its popularity and stability to Āryadēva. But in Āryadēva we find not only criticism of the Theravāda but also of the Sāṃkhya and Vaiśeṣika conceptions. This is done because there was a need to consolidate the Mādhyamika position against the Non-Buddhist systems.

HIS DEATH

Kumārajīva narrates how Āryadēva passed away at the hands of a murderer, who was a pupil of one of the heretical teachers whom Dēva had vanquished in debate.[117] His disciples wanted to take revenge and ran after the murderer, but Āryadēva restrained them with these words: "Everything is unreal in the world. If you recognise the true nature of all things, then there is neither murdered nor murderer. Who is a friend and who is a foe?"[118] This is the essence of Āryadēva's philosophy. He was a great missionary who sacrificed his life for thr propagation of Mahāyāna. Along with Nāgārjuna's *Madhyamaka Śāstra* and *Dvādaśanikāya Śāstra*, Āryadēva's *Catuḥśataka* or *Śataśāstra* forms the ground work of the faith of the 'Sanron' sect in Japan.[119] Āryadēva thus shares the honour of founding the Mādhyamaka system with his master Nāgārjuna. For that, he may be called second Nāgārjuna.[120]

BUDDHAPĀLITA AND BHĀVAVIVEKA

By about the 5th century A.D., the Mādhyamikas were split up into two sects : the Prāsaṅgika and Svātantrika. The sects were founded by Buddhapālita and Bhāvaviveka respectively. Both of them were associated with Āndhradeśa. Though we could gather some information about Bhāvaviveka, very little is known about the life and activities of Buddhapālita. But both of them are known to be the disciples of Saṅgharakṣita.[121]

Buddhapālita is said to have been a native of Dantapura.[122] The place is identified with Kaliṅgapaṭṭaṇam in Chicacole district.[123] It was the capital of ancient Kaliṅga and was called Dantapura in the Ceylonese chronicles as it was connected with the tooth relic that was carried to Ceylon.[124]

Buddhapālita was an ardent follower of Nāgārjuna, and wrote a commentary named Madhyamakavṛtti on Nāgārjuna's Madhyamaka Śāstra. Buddhapālita held prasaṅga to be the real method of Nāgārjuna and Āryadēva.[125] The method is to lead the opponent to an absurd position and prove him wrong. His school therefore came to be known as the Prāsaṅgika school of the Mādhyamika, which is given an exposition in his Madhyamakavṛtti.

Bhāvaviveka was one of the great masters of Mahāyāna śāstra and a reknown dialectician. He wrote in defence of Nāgārjuna and propagated his system. He is known as Bhavya also.

Yuan Chwang gives some information about the nativity and date of Bhāvaviveka.The Chinese pilgrim writes "Bhāvaviveka lived in a place on a mountain cliff or great rock hill not far from the south side of the capital Dhānyakaṭaka"[126] Most of the accounts unanimously state that he was born in a Kṣatriya family of Malayagiri. About 20 miles from Dhānyakaṭaka[127] there is a place Mangalagiri, where there is also a hill. This may be identified with Malayagiri of the above accounts. That Mangalagiri is an ancient place, is proved by inscriptions.[128] After ordination Bhāvaviveka spent most of his life time at Dhānyakaṭaka.

Yuan Chwang holds Bhāvaviveka as a contemporary of Dharmapāla[129] whereas I-tsing places Bhāvaviveka earlier than Dignāga and Dharmapāla.[130] On the basis of these accounts, Winternitz places him in the 5th century A.D., whereas Kimura;[131] and Nakamura[132] place him in the 6th century A.D. Bhāvaviveka is known to have resorted to Madhyadeśa where he became a disciple of Saṅgharakṣita, [133] and studied with him the Mahāyāna texts, particularly the Mādhyamika system of Nāgārjuna.[134] Having returned to his native place, he took care of 50 monasteries and had a large number of disciples.[135]

Bhāvaviveka is credited with the authorship of the following four important works:[136]

1. *Mahāyāna karatālaratna Śāstra*
2. *Mādhyamika hṛdaya tarkajvālā*
3. *Madhyamakārtha saṁgraha*
4. *Prajñā Pradīpa*

The Tibetans ascribe to him four more works:[137]

1. *Pradīpa uddyotana nāma - ṭīkā*
2. *Pañca krama-pañjikā-nāma*
3. *Madhyamakahṛdaya vṛtti tarkajvālā* .
4. *Nikāyabheda vibhaṅga Vyākhyāna*

In his works, Bhāvaviveka gave a clear exposition of a new school of Mādhyamika, famous as the Svātantrika. He rejected Buddhapālita's Prāsaṅgika system and argued that the opponent should not only be reduced to absurdity but independent logical arguments should be advanced to silence him.[138] For the purpose of pin-pointing absolute truth, one can not entirely depend upon dialectics.[139] He stated that śūnyatā was not the denial of the empircal vali dity of things but only their ultimate reality not the assertion of non-existence of things but the dogmatic assertion of existence.[140]

KARATALARATNA

N.Aiyaswami has restored *Karatalaratna* from the Chinese translation of Yuan Chwang into Sanskrit.[141] Poussin has translated it into French. In this work Bhāvaviveka attempts to establish the basic Mādhyamika stand-point by syllogistic arguments.

TARKAJVĀLĀ

The profound scholarship of Bhāvaviveka is revealed

in his Tarkajvālā. In this work he criticised the views of Śaṃkhya, Vaiśēṣika and Vedānta, often quoting from the original texts and expounded the Svātantrika method. In his commentary on Tarkajvālā, Yuan Chwang says that Bhāvaviveka refuted not only the non-Mādhyamika doctrines, Hīnayana as well as Yogācāra[142] but also Brahmanic schools of thought. Bhāvaviveka's knowledge of Sāṃkhya led Yuan Chwang to comment that though Bhavya was an ardent follower of Nāgārjuna, appeared externally as a Sāṃkhya.[143]

PRAJÑĀPRADĪPA

The Prajñāpradīpa is an expository treatise on Nāgārjuna's *Mūla Mādhyamaka Kārikā*. Bhāvaviveka is said to have also written an independent work - *Madhyamakāvatārapradīpa* and another Prakaraṇa: *Madhyamakapratītyasamutpāda.*[144]

MADHYAMAKĀRTHA SAṂGRAHA

Aiyaswami Sastri restored the text into Sanskrit and published in Journal of Oriental Research, Madras.[145] In this, Bhavya maintains that the Buddhist sutras which contain the words of the Buddha are the only authority and independent source of knowledge. They need no verification by reason. In the beginning, the Mādhyamika stand-point is maintained as the true teaching on rational and textual grounds but gradually dialectical criticism also was held inadequate and Svātantrika or speculative tendency was developed.[146]

DIGNĀGA

Not only Madhyamaka shcool but also Vijñānavāda

school had followers in Āndhradeśa. One of the greatest Vijñānavāda writers who lived in Andhra was Dignāga,[147] "He was master mind" and one of the foremost figures in the history of Indian philosophy. He was a disciple of Vasubandhu. Dignāga was mostly an independent thinker among his sccessors. Dignāga was regarded as the father of Buddhist logic. He was a great celebrity in disputations with opponents, Dignāga became one of the most powerful propagators of Buddhism.

Most scholars are of the view that Dignāga lived about the 6th century A.D.[148] The general consensus among scholars is that he was born at Kanchi.[149] But the Tibetan tradition says that he was born at Siṁhavaktra near Kanchi.[150] Siṁhavaktra is identified with Vikramasiṁhapura of Nellore.[151] The Tibetan tradition further says that he lived on Bhoraśaila in Orissa, [152] whereas Yuan Chwang associates him with Āndhra.[153]

There might be truth in both the traditions as the regions are contiguous. The account of Yuan Chwang is that he saw a Saṅghārāma on a hill 200 li further south-west of Ping-ki-lo (Vengi), the capital of An-to-lo (Āndhra). On the ridge of this isolated hill was a stone tope where Dignāga (Channa) Pūsa lived and composed a treatise on logic. That Vengi is no doubt a Buddhist Kṣetra, is established by the recent discovery of the ruins of a big stūpa and other antiquities.[154] However, Guṇṭupalli, where there are a rock-cut caitya and vihāra answers well the description of Yuan Chwang.[155] Therefore it may be concluded that Dignāga spent the most useful part of his life in Āndhradeśa. Tradition says that Mañjuśrī summoned him to develop for the benefit of posterity the "*Yogā cārabhūmi śāstra*" originally delivered by Maitreya.[156]

CAREER AND WORKS

Dignāga was converted to Buddhism at an early age by a teacher of the Vātsiputrīya sect and took the vows from him. But on certain points he could not agree with his teacher and left his monastery. Later he became the disciple of Vasubandhu and in the study of the science of logic he advanced further and attained great fame. Dignāga largely lived in Āndhradeśa and travelled in Mahārāṣtra and Orissa, controverting the Tīrthikas.[157] In course of time, he converted a minister of the king of Orissa[158] and founded sixteen Mahāvihāras.[159] Later, Dignāga passed away in a forest in Orissa. After his death, his pupils founded schools and carried on the study of his works. Ēśvarasena and Śankaraswāmin, the celebrated logicians were the direct pupils of Dignāga.

According to I-tsing, 'this star of the first magnitude in logic was the author of 100 treatises.' The *Pramāṇa Samuccaya* is the greatest of his works and it is believed to have been composed near Vengi. It was the earliest work on modern pure Nyāya which developed Pramāṇa or evidence as means of knowledge.[160] It was Dignāga who separated logic from disputation and replaced the word Vāda by Nyāya.[161] At first he gave exposition to his ideas in a series of short tracts, some of which are preserved in Tibetan and Chinese translations.[162] Later the tracts were condensed into the *Pramāṇasamuccaya* in six chapters in verse with the author's own commentary.[163] Later Jinendra Buddhi composed a good commentary on it called *Viśālāmalavatī.*[164]

Other fragmentary works of Dignāga on logic are: (1) *Ālambana Parīkṣa*[165] (2) *Trikāla Parīkṣa*[166] (3) *Hetucakra ḍamaru*[167] (4) *and Nyāyamukha (Dvāra).*[168] I-Tsing furnishes us with the titles of eight works of Dignāga, which were used by students as text books on logic. Stcherbatsky says that in Dignāga "One finds a comprehensive system of critical philosophy".[169] Some of his works were rendered into Chinese by Paramārtha in the 6th Century A.D. He is therefore rightly regarded as the father of Indian logic, more correctly, of Buddhist logic.[170]

Besides a number of works on logic, Dignāga composed *Prajñā Pāramitā Saṁgraha or Prajñā Pāramitā Piṇḍārtha.*[171] in which he expressed his views on the theory of Advaya.[172] Haribhadra quotes his works twice in his Abhisamayālaṅkāraloka.[173] Tucci has published the entire work with an English translation.[174] In this Dignāga says that Prajñāpāramitā (highest wisdom) is non-dual knowledge and that is the Tathāgata.

His system shows an admixture of Sautrāntika and Vijñānavāda tenets and he is known to have criticised Naiyāyika logical theories. With him therefore begins a new epoch in the history of Buddhist thought and in that of Indian philosophy.[175] Later the Buddhist thinkers began to take an active part in philosophical debates and a keen interest in logical theories.[176]

Dignāga is said to have controverted Īśvara Kṛṣṇa the author of the Sānkhya Kārikā[177] and defeated a Brāhmaṇa logician named Sudurjaya in a religious debate.[178] He subjected Vātsyāyana also to criticism.[179] On the other hand, Dignāga was criticised by the most famous Buddhist thinkers like Chandrakīrti, [180] and by Brāhmanists such as Udyotakara, Kumārilabhaṭṭa and Pārthasāradhimiśra.[181] However this great logician doubted the efficacy of logic in fully grasping the Dharma.[182]

DHARMAKĪRTI

Dharmakīrti may be said to have been the last great Mahāyāna philosopher that lived in Āndhradeśa. He was a great exponent of Yogācāra school. The accounts of his life as given by Tārānātha and Buston are overlaid with incredible mythological elements and it is very difficult to sift the grains of historical truths from them. Scholars are agreed that Dharmakīrti was a native of Tirumala in the kingdom of Cūḍāmaṇi.[183] Tirumala, is no other than the present-day Tirumala-Tirupati, a great Hindu pilgrim centre in Chittur district of Āndhra Pradesh.

The date of Dharmakīrti can be determined with the help of the clue provided by the Chinese traveller I-tsing.[184] He says that Dharmakīrti, the great logician after Dignāga "flourished in recent years", when lived Dharmapāla and Śīlabhadra. Śīlabhadra and Dharmakīrti may have been class fellows under Dharmapāla.[185] Śīlabhadra was the Chancellor of the University of Nalanda in or about 635 A.D., when Yuan Chwang first visited the University. But Yuan Chwang does not mention Dharmakīrti. Rahul Samkrityayana explains this silence of Yuan Chwang about the Dharmakīrti that the latter might have died before the Chinese traveller visited Nalanda or India.[186]

On the basis of Tibetan sources, Stcherbatsky places Dharmakīrti in the middle of the 7th century A.D.[187] Buston says that Īśvarasena one of Dignāga's pupils was the teacher of Dharmakīrti.[188] The Blue Annals record the follwoing lineage of teachers: Vasubandhu, Dignāga, Īśvarasena and Dharmakīrti.[189] This is also the line of succession given by Buston. Therefore Dharmakīrti, a direct pupil of Īśvarasena may be placed between 580-650 A.D. Dharmakīrti seems to have studied Vijñānavāda under Dharmapāla and *Pramāṇasamuccaya* under Īśvarasena.[190]

Tārānātha records that Dharmakīrti was a contemporary of Sron btsan sgam po, king of Tibet and therefore Dharmakīrti should have lived in the first half of the 7th century A.D.[191]

Buston writes that Kumārila the heritical teacher, was the uncle of Dharmakīrti.[192] This tradition is corroborated by Tārānātha[193] and Sumpā mkhan po. According to Tārānatha and Sumpā mkhan, Kumārila was defeated by Dharmakīrti in debate and as a result the former accepted Buddhism along with his five hundred followers.[194] The *Śankara - Digvijaya* of Mādhava also records that Kumārila was defeated and converted by Dharmakīrti.[195]

Dr. S.C.Vidyabhusan was the first to express the view that Dharmakīrti and Uddyotakara were contemporaries and that the latter who was the author of *Nyāyavārtika* had quoted and criticised the ideas of Dharmakīrti.[196] Dharmakīrti seems to have survived Uddyotakara, and became famous for his poetical compositions as well during the first quarter of the 7th century A.D.

Buston refers to Dharmakīrti's special training in grammar.[197] Tārānātha attributes a verse to him in which Dharmakīrtị boasts to have surpassed Chandragomin in grammer and Āryasūra in poetry.[198] The commentaries on the Jatakamālā by Dharmakīrti, still extant in Tibetan[199] may have been among those prized by Harsha, whose date coincides with that of Dharmakīrti.

CAREER

Dharmakīrti was a Brāhmin by birth. He received

brāhmanical education. He then became interested in Buddhism and became an Upāsaka. He received instruction from a direct pupil of Vasubandhu. Then he had been to Nalanda and met Dharmapāla who was very old and from him he took the vows. Later he became the disciple of Īśvarasena. As a person, Dharmakīrti was very proud and self-reliant and had a contempt for sham scholars.[200] By the time of Dharmakīrti, Buddhism was on the decline and Hinduism was becoming popular. He was at one stage grieved by the absence of persons who could fully understand his system and to whom the contribution of his work could have been entrusted.

Tārānātha tells us that when he finished his great work he showed it to the Paṇḍits, but he met with no appreciation and no good will. He bitterly complained of their slow wits and their envy. His enemies, it is reported, then tied up the leaves of his work to the tail of a dog and let him run through the streets where the leaves became scattered. Dharmakīrti remarked "just as the dog runs through all streets so will my work be spread in all the world".[201] Later, Dharmakīrti died in Kalinga in a monastery founded by himself.[202]

The following works are attributed to Dharmakīrti: (1) Pramāṇa Vārttikā, (2) Pramāṇa Viniscaya, (3) Nyāya Biṅdu, (4) Hetu Biṅdu, (5) Sambaṅdha Parīkṣa, and (6) Codana Prakaraṇa.

Pramāṇa Vārttikā

The *Pramāṇavārttika* is the greatest of the works attributed to Dharmakīrti. It is not only a commentary on Dignāga's work, *Pramāṇa-samuccaya*, but is an original explanation of elements of logic and critical philosophy.[203] This work was recently discovered in Tibet by Rahul

Sankrityayana. Until the discovery of this work, Dharmakīrti's pre-eminence as a logician was not recognised in India.[204] He represents the culmination of the Buddha's dynamic philosophy, in which Buddha is conceived as "Embodied logic" (Pramāṇabhūta).[205]

The Tibetan tradition attributes to Dharmakīrti three more works. They are a poetical work, commentary on Ārya Sūra's Jātakamālā and Vinaya-sūtra.[206]

According to Rahul Sankrityayana, Dharmakīrti was never excelled by any one in his critical reasoning, bold analysis and clear thinking.[207] Buston says that even his contemporary heretical paṇḍitas were convinced of the subtlety and excellence of Dharmakīrti's intellectual powers and treatises.[208]

A king of Vindhyan region who was an admirer of this philosopher Dharmakīrti is reported to have inscribed on a slab on his royal gate the follwoing lines: "If Dharmakīrti, the sun among disputants, sets and his doctrines sleep or die, the false doctrines of the Tīrthikas will then rise."[209]

The Tibetan tradition says that Ācārya Nāgārjuna, Āryadeva, Asaṅga Vasubandhu, Dignāga and Dharmakīrti are the six Jewels that adorned Bhārata-varṣa. It is interesting that four of them were associated with Āndhra and this clearly establishes the contribution of Āndhra deśa to Buddhist Philosophy in particular and Indian culture in general.

REFERENCES

1. N.Dutt, Aspects of Mahāyāna and its relation to Hīnayāna, (London, 1930), p. 43.
2. T.R.V.Murti, The Central Philosophy of Buddhism, (London, 1980), p. 4

3. *Ibid*, p. 107.
4. R.Kimura, *Historical study of the terms Hīnayāna and Mahāyāna and the origin of Mahāyāna Buddhism*. (Delhi 1978) p. 169
5. P.S.Sastri, 'Some Buddhist Thinkers of Āndhra', I.H.Q., Vol. XXXII, p. 164
6. *Ibid*.
7. K.R.Subramanian, *Buddhist Remains in Āndhra and the History of South India*, (Waltair, 1932), pp. 60-62.
8. Debi Prasad Chattopadhyaya (Ed.) *Tārānāthas, History of Buddhism in India*, (Calcutta, 1980), p. 228.
9. T.R.V.Murty, op. cit., p. 95.
10, *Ibid*.
11. K.Satchidananda Murty, *Nāgārjuna* (Delhi, 1983) p. 10. (Reprint).
12. Sir Charles Eliot, *Hinduism and Buddhism*, (London, 1962), Vol.I., p. XXXII.
13. T.Watters, *On yuan chwang travels in India*, (Delhi, 1961), p. 203.
14. K.R.Subramanian, op. cit, p. 62.
15. Aiyappan A. and P.R. Srinivasan, *Story of Buddhism with special refernce to South India*, Dept of information and publicity Govt. of Madras, Madras. 1960, p. 28.
16. K. Satchidananda Murty, *Nāgārjuna*, p. 40.
17. *Ibid*, p. 42.
18. G.V.Krishna Rao, *Vigrahavyāvartanī*, (Telugu) Introduction, (Tenali, 1964).
19. It is a long established tradition in Āndhradeśa to have village names as family names. In the Godāvari (East) district, there is a brāhmin family who have Vedula' as their family name. It is possible that they originally hailed from Vedali, which may be located in the region of Palnāḍu, on the basis of the Tibetan accounts.
20. L.M.Joshi, *Life and time of Mādhyamika Philosopher Nāgārjuna. The Mahābodhi*. (Calcutta, 1965), Vol.73, Nos.1 & 2, p. 44.
21. Naropa, The great Vajrayāna authority of the 10th Century A.D. uses the word Śrī Dhānya twice in his Sekoddeśaṭīkā, L.M.Joshi, 'Original Home of Tāntric Buddhism', Journal of Oriental Institute, Vol. xvi (1967), p. 223. ff.
22. K.Satchidananda Murty, op. cit. p. 43.

23. Richard Robinson, *Early Mādhyamika in India and China*, (Delhi, 1976), p. 24.
24. *Ibid.*
25. Winternitz, *History of Indian Literature* (Delhi, 1977), Vol.II. p. 342.
26. T.R.V.Murty, op. cit. p. 88.
27. Suniti Kumara Pathak, "Life of Nāgārjuna", I.H.Q., xxx, p. 93.
28. M.A.S.I., No.71, p. 28.
29. K.Satchidananda Murty, op. cit. pp. 13-14.
30. M.A.S.I., No.71, p. 29.
31. B.S.L.Hanumantha Rao, *Religion in Āndhra,* Appendix 4, pp. 326-327.
32. D.C.Sircar, H.C.I.P., II, p. 203/
33. B.S.L. Hanumantha Rao, "Contemporaneity of Kanishka and Nāgārjuna Examined", J.A.H.R.S., XVI, p. 23 ff.
34. S.Beal, Indian Antiquary, IX, pp. 148-149.
35. E.J.Thomas, *The History of Buddhist Thought*, (London, 1963), p. 176.
36. Winternitz, op. cit., p. 342.
37. Rājataranginī, 1, 173 ff., Quoted from Winternitz.
38. C.Śivarāma Murty, *Amarāvati Sculptures in Madras Government Museum*, (Madras, 1977), p. 12.
39. G.V.Krishna Rao, op. cit.
40. B.S.Upadhyaya, In *2500 years of Buddhism*, p. 22.
41. K.A.Nilakanta Sastri, *Foreign Notices of South India*, (Madras, 1939), p. 97.
42. E.I. Vol.VIII. (1905-1906), p. 60.
43. E.I., XXXVI, p. 273.
44. B.S.L. Hanumantha Rao, op. cit,
45. G.V.Krishna Rao, op. cit.
46. E.I., Vol.XXXVI, p. 273 ff.
47. Richard Robinson, *Early Mādhyamika in India and China*, p. 21.
48. K.Satchidananda Murty, *Nāgārjuna*, p. 41.
49. *Ibid*,
50. K.V.Ramana, *Nāgārjuna's Philosophy-Introduction.*
51. *Story of Buddhism with Special reference to South India*, p. 118.
52. J.Ph.Vogel, *Indian Serpent Lore*, (London.1926), p. 34.
53. Watters, *On Yuan Chwang Travells in India*, (Delhi, 1961), p. 204.

54. E.I., Vol.XXXVI, p. 273.
55. E.I., vol. xx, p. 1.
56. E.I., Vol.VIII, p. 61.
57. E.I., Vol.XX, "Nāgārjunakoṇḍa inscriptions", F.
58. R.Kimura, "Mahāyāna and Hīnayāna works known to Nāgārjuna", I.H.Q., III, p. 40
59. H.Kern, *Manual of Indian Buddhism,* (Delhi, 1972), p. 6. and p. 123.
60. Max Welleser, Life of Nāgārjuna quoted by K.V.Ramana, op. cit. p. 1.
61. Charles Eliot, *Hinduism and Buddhism,* Vol.III, p. 219.
62. *Kathāsaritsāgara*, Taraṅga -41, p. 174 ff.
63. K.A.Nilakanta Sastri, op. cit., p. 97.
64. Richard Robinson, op. cit., pp. 26-27.
65. Winternitz, op. cit., p. 344.
66. *Ibid.*
67. K.V.Ramana, *Nāgārjuna's Philosophy*, (Delhi, 1978), Introduction, p. 25.
68. T.R.V.Murti, op. cit., p. 83.
69. *Ibid.*
70. Jayadev Singh, op. cit., p. 9.
71. *Ibid*, p. 10.
72. *Ibid*, p. 9.
73. P.S.Sastri, "Nāgārjuna and Āryadēva", *Studies in the History of Indian Philosophy*, Vol.III. (Calcutta, 1979), p. 190.
74. Winternitz, op. cit. p. 348.
75. *Ibid*, p. 36.
76. *Ibid.*
77. Giuseppe Tucci, J.R.A.S., 1934, pp. 308-325, 1936, pp. 238-252, and 1936, pp. 424-435.
78. Michael Hahn, *Nāgārjuna's Ratnāvalī,* Vol.I, *The Basic Texts*, (Bonn, 1982).
79. Ratnāvalī, IV, 70.
80. *Ibid*, 81.
81. *Ibid*, 37.
82. Winternitz, op. cit, p. 347.
83. Takakusu, I-Tsing, (Oxford, 1896), pp. 158-62.
84. Richard Robinson, *Dvādaśanikāya Śāstra,* (Holland, 1982), p. 54.
85. *Ibid.*

86. E.R.E., Vol.VIII, 235 ff, & E.R.E., Vol.IV, p. 838.
87. T.R.V.Murti, *The Central Philosophy of Buddhism*, p. 87.
88. Winternitz, op. cit., pp. 348-349.
89. *Encyclopaedia of Buddhism*, Vol.I, p. 109.
90. Buston's, *History of Buddhism*, (Tr.) Ober Miller Vol.II (Heidelbarg, 1932) p. 130.
91. P.S.Sastri, "Some Buddhist Thinkers of Āndhradeśa", I.H.Q., Vol.XXXII, p. 164.
92. Debi Prasad Chattopadhyaya (Ed.), *Tārānātha's History of Buddhism in India*, (Calcutta, 1980), p. 124.
93. K.Satchidananada Murty, Contribution of Āndhra to Buddhist Thought, Dr. S.Radhakrishnan Memorial Lecture, I.T.I., (Hyderabad, 1980), p. 20.
94. Richard Robinson, *Early Mādhyamika in India and China*, (Delhi, 1976), p. 27.
95. T.Watters op. cit., vol. II, p. 320. (Modern Nellore was originally called Vikramasimhapura).
96. P.S.Sastri, op. cit., p. 164.
97. *Ibid.*
98. *Ibid.*
99. B.S.L.Hanumantha Rao, *The Age of Sātavāhanas*, (Hyderabad, 1976), p. 4.
100. P.S.Sastri, op. cit., p. 164.
101. P.S.Sastri, "Nāgārjuna and Āryadēva", *Studies in the History of Indian Philosophy*, Vol.III, (Ed.) by Debi Prasad Chattopadhyaya (Calcutta, 1979), p. 186.
102. *Ibid.*
103. K.Satchidananada Murty, op. cit., p. 21.
104. Richard Robinson, op. cit, pp. 27-28.
105. S.Beal in, *Indian Antiquary*, Vol.IX, pp. 148-149.
106. Watters, T, op. cit., p. 245.
107. S.Beal, *The Life of Yuan Chwang*, (Delhi, 1973), p. 135.
108. T.R.V.Murty, op. cit., pp. 92-95.
109. Robinson, op. cit., pp. 27-29.
110. T.R.V.Murty, op. cit., p. 93.
111. *Ibid*, p. 94.
112. *Ibid*, p. 93.
113. Winternitz, op. cit., p. 351.
114. *Ibid.*

115. Watters, T. *On Yuan Chwang's Travels of India*, p. 320-21.
116. K.R.Subrāmanian, *Buddhist ramains in Āndhradeśa and the History of South India* (Waltair, 1932), p. 62.
117. Winternitz, op. cit., 349.
118. *Encyclopaedia of Buddhism*, p. 144.
119. Winternitz, M. *Studies in the History of Indian Literature*, (Delhi, 1978), p. 349.
120. *Ibid*, p. 351.
121. N.Dutt in Classical Age, p. 358.
122. *Ibid*.
123. Alexander Cunningham, The Ancient Geography of India, (Delhi, 1975), p. 436.
124. Turnour, Daladavaṁsa, Journal of Asiatic Society of Bengal, 1837, p. 860.
125. T.R.V.Murty, op. cit., p. 95.
126. S.Beal, *The Life of Yuan-Chwang*, (London, 1914), p. 95.
127. S. •Beal, *Buddhist Records of the Western World*, (Delhi, 1983), p. 223.
128. E.I. Vol.XXXV, Nāgārjunakoṇḍa Inscriptions, pp. 15-16.
129. K.R.Subramanian, op. cit., p. 62.
130. *Ibid*.
131. R.Kimura, Op. cit, pp. 184-185.
132. K.Satchidananda Murty, op. cit., p. 22.
133. N.Dutt, *Classical age*, p. 387.
134. *Ibid*.
135. *Ibid*.
136. K.R.Subrāmaṇian, op. cit., p. 62.
137. Debiprasad Chattopadhyay (Ed.) *Tārānātha's History of Buddhism in India* (Calcutta, 1980), p. 401.
138. T.R.V.Murti, op. cit., p. 95.
139. *Ibid*.
140. *Ibid*, p. 97.
141. N.Aiyaswami Sastri, *Karatalaratna*, quoted by T.R.V.Murti, p. 96.
142. L.M.Joshi, op. cit. p. 8.
143. Watters, T. Vol-II, op. cit, p. 215.
144. T.R.V.Murti, op. cit. p. 98.
145. *Ibid*, pp. 98 and p. 243. F.N.4.
146. K.Satchidananda Murty, op. cit, p. 22.
147. P.S.Sastri, op. cit., p. 165.

148. L.M.Joshi, *Studies in the Buddhistic Cultures of India*, (Delhi, 1967), p. 8.
149. P.V.Bapat, (Ed.) *2500 years of Buddhism*, p. 225.
150. Tārānātha's *History of Buddhism in India*, op. cit, p. 181.
151. P.S.Sastri, op. cit. p. 165.
152. Taranatha's, *History of Buddhism in India*, op. cit. p. 182, f.n.1.
153. S.Beal, *Buddhist Records of the Western World*, (Delhi, 1983), pp. 217-220.
154. I.K.Sarma, Pedavegi, "Dhanamdibba" 1986, *Bharati*, (Telugu monthly), Jan.1987.
155. A.H.Longhurst, "The Buddhist Monuments at Guntupalli, Krishna district", A.R.A.S. (Southern Circle) 1916-17, (March, 1917), pp. 30-36.
156. Watters, T. *On Yuanchwang Travels in Indian*, Vol-II, pp. 209-210.
157. K.R.Subramaniyan, op. cit, p. 63.
158. Taranath's *History of Buddhism in India*, op. cit. pp. 184-185.
159. *Ibid*, p. 185.
160. K.R.Subramaniyan, op. cit. p. 63.
161. Stecherbatsky, "Dignāga and Dharmakīrti", *Studies in the History of Indian Philosophy*, Vol.III, (Calcuttta, 1979), p263.
161. *Ibid.*
162. *Ibid.*
163. *Ibid.*
164. *Ibid.*
165. *Ibid.*
166. H.N.Randle, *Fragments from Dignāga*, (Delhi, 1981), pp. 1-8.
167. *Ibid.*
168. P.V.Bapat, (Ed.) 2500 Years of Buddhism, p. 225.
169. Stcherbatsky, *Buddhist Logic*, (Hague, 1958), Vol.I. pp. 31, 32.
170. N.Dutt, in *Classical Age*, p. 391.
171. Winternitz, op. cit., p. 363 f.n.
172. Stcherbatsky, op. cit. p. 31.
173. Haribadra, "*Abhisamayālaṅkārāloka*", in J.R.A.S. 1947, pp. 21-153.
174. *Ibid*, pp. 53-75.
175. Stcherbatsky, op. cit., p. 59, f.
176. Edward Conze, *Buddhist Thought in India*, (London, 1962), p. 265.
177. Stcherbatsky, "Dignāga and Dharmakīrti"; op. cit., p. 263.

178. 2500 Years of Buddhism, p. 225.
179. P.S.Sastri, "Some Buddist thinkers of Andhradesa" I.H.Q. Vol.XXXII, p. 165.
180. *Ibid.*
181. N.Dutt, Classical Age, p. 390.
182. K.Satchidananda Murty, op. cit., p. 23.
183. Taranatha's, *History of Buddhism in India*, op. cit. p. 228.
184. Takakusu, I-Tsing, (Oxford, 1896), pp. 181-82.
185. R.C.Majumdar (Ed.) Classical Age, p. 383.
186. L.M.Joshi, op. cit., p. 427.
187. Stcherbatsky, *Buddhist Logic*, Vol.I, pp. 29-30.
188. Buston, Vol.II. p. 152.
189. George N. Roerich, *Blue Annals*, Vol.I, (Delhi, 1979), p. 346. (Resprint).
190. L.M.Joshi, op. cit. p. 428.
191. *Ibid*, p. 184.
192. Buston, Vol.II, p. 152.
193. Taranatha, op. cit. p. 230.
194. L.M.Joshi, *Studies in the Buddhistic Cultures of India*, (Delhi, 1967), p. 429.
195. *Ibid*, p. 430.
196. *Ibid*, p. 433.
197. Buston, Vol.II, pp. 151-52.
198. L.M.Joshi, op. cit, p. 184.
199. *Ibid*, p. 435.
200. Stcherbatsky, "Dignāga and Dharmakīrti", *History of Indian Philosophy*, Vol.III, pp. 266-267.
201. Buston, Vol.II, p. 154.
202. Stcherbatsky, op. cit, p. 226.
203. *Ibid.*
204. Stcherbatsky, *Buddhist Logic*, Vol.I., p. 38.
205. Vidyabhusana, *History of Indian Logic*, (Calcutta, 1921, p. 307.
206. L.M.Joshi, op. cit. p. 184.
207. *Ibid*, p. 185.
208. Buston. Vol.II, p. 154.
209. L.M.Joshi, op. cit., p. 185.

CHAPTER-IV

IMPACT OF MAHĀYĀNA ON LIFE AND SOCIETY

For about 300 years Mahāyāna exerted profound influence on the social and cultural life of Āndhras. No doubt it had fulfilled the expectations of its exponents. As observed already, its emergence was the result of the reconciliation of Buddhism with the local religious sentiments and practices. Mahāyāna has further removed the differences between parivrājaka and upāsaka by holding that household life was no hindrance to spriritual exercises leading to Nirvāṇa. As a result Mahāyāna succeeded in holding large sections of people to the bosom of Buddhism. T.N.Ramachandran remarks that "the vast population of Buddhist monks of the place only shows unmistakably the great popularity of the religion amongst the people[1]."

The popularity of the religion is revealed by the large number of Buddhist sites discovered all over Āndhra. The names like Hugha, [2] Roha, [3] Sujātā[4], Chadakā[5], wife of Ahubuddhi, [6] Siddhārthanikā, [7] Bodhi, [8] Buddhila, [9] Buddhi, [10] ascetic Uttarā, [11] Saṅghala, [12] Buddharakkhitā, [13] Bodhisiri, [14] Buddhavanikina, [15] Bodhi Śarma, [16] Buddhavanīya, [17] Saṅghadāsī, [18] Haghasiri[19] etc., we come across in donaṭory records reveal the love and admiration of the people for Buddhism. As the artisan and merchant communities who were the chief patrons of Buddhism were also the back bone of state economy at that time, the rulers of the age should have felt it impolitic to antagonise these sections by being hostile to Buddhism.[20] That may be mentioned as one of the reasons for the tolerant attitude of the Sātavāhanas and Ikṣvākus towards Buddhism, though they were stout champions of Brāhmanism.

Inspite of the reformation of Brāhmanism through Bhāgavatism and temple building activity from about 275 A.D..[21] at Vijayapuri Buddhism could command the loyalty of people in general. Brāhmanism received patronage only from kings and their loyal officers and we rarely come across popular gifts to Brāhmanical temples during this period, whereas people in general, merchants, artisans and ladies including those of the harem continued to patronise Buddhism as evidenced by inscriptions.

SOCIETY

The Buddhist Saṅgha did not recognise caste while the Brāhmanical social order was based upon it. During this period when Buddhism enjoyed wide popularity, people appear to have been not conscious of their varṇa or caste. Though Gautamīputra Sātakarṇi claimed to have stopped the admixture of four castes[22] (Vinivartita cāturvarṇa sankarasya) as his titles suggest, that caste did not become rigid is indicated by his son marrying a Śāka princess.[23] Another of Gautamīputra's title dvijavara kuṭuṁba vivardhana[24] (promoter of Brāhmin families) would suggest that earlier, the Brāhmins did not enjoy a predominant position. But even afterwards, the Brāhmins did not gain prominence in society is indicated by vaiśyas holding high positions at the court. Vishṇugupta, probably a vaiśya was the minister of Gautamīputra Sātakarṇi. The people were usually accustomed to mention only their occupations but not castes.[25]. Only two of the Ikṣvāku records make reference to Brāhmins. The inscription of the chāyāstambha[26] of Koḍārakā says that he was respected both by the Brāhmins and Śramaṇas or Buddhist monks. Another inscription issued by Cāṁtisiri[27] says that she bestowed matchless gifts on Brāhmins and Śramaṇas. There is only indirect evidence to the important position which the Brāhmins occupied as the custodians of Brāhmanical lore and tradition.[28]

Large number of artisans, merchants and women embraced Buddhism and patronised its institutions. The construction of the stūpas and vihāras was almost a community work, each devotee gifting one part of the structure or the other. Of all such donations, the most remarkable is the one made by a cobbler by name Vidhika.[29] Vidhika was the son of Nāga, who was a teacher or Upājjhāya. He visited the stūpa and made a gift of a slab with pūrṇa ghaṭa. He was accompanied to the place by his mother, wife, brother, sons, daugherts, cousins, relations and friends. No other instance than this is needed to explain the popular nature of Āndhra Buddhism, and the cosmopolitan spirit of the Buddhist institutions. Kumārilabhaṭṭa might be right when he said in his *Tantravārtikā*[30] that Buddhism appealed to those who were outside the pale of the Varṇas who mostly comprised the fouth or the low caste.

CONDITION OF THE WOMEN

As Mahāyāna did not insist upon monasticism, women appear to have preferred Buddhism. Large number of gifts to Buddhist Sangha during this period were made by royal ladies and common folk. Women of this period, as indicated by the records enjoyed much economic freedom. It appears that they had property of their own. From the inscriptions we gather that the ladies of the Ikṣvāku family got the Mahācaitya in the Nāgārjunakoṇḍa renovated at great cost.[31] They constructed many vihāras and caitya halls. The inscriptions found in association with the Mahācaitya of Nāgārjunakoṇḍa show that various parts of the monument were gifted by women of middle class also. One of such ladies was Bodhiśiri[32] who was a lady disciple who constructed shrines, caityas, maṇḍapas, and cells at different places like Kaṇṭakaśila, Hiramuthuva, Papila, Puṣpagiri and Devagiri for the benefit of the Buddhist community. In one of the Amarāvati sculptures we find depicted a disputation between two scholars and the audience consists mostly of women.[33]

Some of the inscriptions from Amarāvati reveal that women were properly educated and served even as teachers. This is evident from one of the Amarāvati inscriptions which says that Mūlā upāsikā[34] is a disciple of the female teacher Samudiyā (upādhyāyanī). Another inscription[35] mentions a lady Navakammikā, Superintendent of New works. Even in the practice of religion and in aiming at spirirtual development, women did not lag behind men. Another inscription from Amarāvati records the gift of a nun Rohā and she is described as passed beyond the eight worldly conditions.[36] She is the daughter of the venerable Sujātā of great self-control. The eight worldly conditions are: gain, loss, respect, contempt, good luck, bad luck, praise and blame.[37] Among the composers of the Gāthās of Saptaśati, there were many poetesses.[38]

SELFLESS SOCIAL CONSCIOUSNESS

In Mahāyāna the extreme individualism of the original Buddhism was replaced by universalism. The Mahāyānists developed selfless social morality based on the practice of positive moral virtues. They laid emphasis on the welfare and happiness of the entire world. In inscriptions Buddha is described as having been inspired by the idea of the happiness and welfare of the entire mankind[39] and as one having compassion for all sentient beings.[40] These descriptions are consistent with the idea of Mahākārunika Bodhisattva. At Nāgārjunakoṇḍa we find sculptures of Bodhisattva in the Triyatriṃśa heaven before his birth as Siddhārtha Gautama.[41] There are several inscriptions recovered from Āndhra Buddhist centres which record such a noble concept. The donors showed a readiness to share the merit of their gifts and other pious deeds with their relations or with the rest of mankind.[42] The principle of transfer of merit became popular with them. For example, a pious devotee donated a chief monastery and a hospital *vigatajvarālaya* with an interest in the welfare of others.[43] (vipulārtha kānkṣin). Gifts were made for the health, victory, prosperity and longevity of their kith and kin.[44] Mahāyāna laid emphasis on the welfare and happiness of the entire world, its motto was "Bahujana Sukhāya" and "Bahujana hitāya". This Mahāyāna religious thought might have influenced even the Hindus which reflects in their ideal "*Sarve-janāḥ Sukhino-bhavantu*.

IMPACT ON ECONOMY

The criticism that Buddhism tended to produce laziness among people and hindered the economic development of the land cannot be taken at its face value.

The Mahāyāna permitted the enjoyment of worldly pleasures within the frame-work of Dharma. This non-rejection of worldly life and the advocacy in favour of lay worshippers gave in fact a fresh stimulus to economic activity in the land. Agriculture received unprecedented encouragement which was beneficial to the gahapati class. The inscriptions mention various artisans who were responsible for the development of different industries. Ptolemy, the Greek geographer, notes the prosperous condition of textile industry in the Maisolia region.[45].

In the inscriptions we frequently come across Vaṇijas[46] who might be of the vaiśya caste. The innumerable gifts of the vaṇijas and their ladies given to the Buddhist establishments reveal that they were the richest and the most prosperous section of the society.

The artisans, merchants and gahapatis or the landed gentry who were rich, played a dominant role in society. Internal and maritime trade expanded. Vijayapuri, Dhānyakaṭaka, Bhaṭṭiprolu, Ghaṇṭasāla and Tamrāpa appear to have been flourishing centres of trade. The inscriptions of Guṇṭupalli[47] and Ghaṇṭasāla[48] mention Mahānāvikas. One of the Uppuguṇḍūru inscription[49] mentions Samudanikā and Sāgaraṁnikā, as names of two ladies of a vaṇija family. These names indicate the intimacy of the vaṇijas with the sea and the veneration they had for it. Much of the maritime trade appears to have been with the Roman empire. Most of the above trading centres yielded Roman gold coins, Roman pottery and other traces of Roman contacts.[50] Rice[51] and probably textiles were exported from the ports on the Āndhra Coast. As Longhurst points out it was the wealth of these communities that had gone into the building of the huge stūpa and vihāra complexes.[52]

It was probably during this period that Buddhism travelled to the far eastern lands including Burma[53] where Āndhra merchant colonies sprang up. Along with Buddhism, traditions of Āndhra art had travelled to those far off lands.[54] It was thus a glorious period of economic prosperity leading to commercial and colonial enterprise and civilising missionary activity in the history of Āndhras which reads almost like a romance.

LITERARY ACTIVITY

Even those who took to monastic discipline did not idle away their time. They acted as teachers, writers and exponents of Buddhist thought and practice. During the period of transition from Mahāsāṅghika to Mahāyāna as mentioned earlier, the Andhakas realised the need of bringing out the deeper meaning of the teachings of the Buddha to save the religion from the onslaught of the reformed Brāhmanism. As noted above, large quantities of Sūtra literature were produced in the vihāras of Āndhradeśa.[55] They were the result of the collective intellectual effort and elaborate discusions carried on by the monks in the vihāras of the Kṛṣṇā valley. Thus philosophical sūtra literature became for Mahāyāna what the Upaniṣads have been for the later philosophy of Vedānta.[56] At the same time, the Vihāras became the seats of individual philosophers like Nāgārjuna, Āryadēva, Bhavya, Dharmakīrti and others who composed commentaries on the Sūtras.

The philosophers mentioned above not only composed commentaries on the original sūtras but composed original works basing upon them. In the course of this effort Nāgārjuna introduced the Kārikā system[57] which was the sūtra and Bhāṣya by the same author. This style has been later adopted in composing most of the scientific treatises. Nāgārjuna is followed by a galaxy of Mahāyāna philosophers whose contributions to philosophy and literature have been described in the above pages. Nāgārjuna's Suhṛllekhā and Ratnāvalī occupy a high place even in secular literature as they contain the philosopher's views and recommendations on several aspects of secular life, especially social ethics and political institutions. In his Suhṛllekhā,[58] Nāgārjuna advises his royal friend:

(1) Understand food to be like medicine neither use it with hatred, not attachment nor for pride or beauty but solely for maintaining body;[59]

(2) Avoid those three kinds of wives: one who, like an executioner, is naturally associated with the enemy; one who like a queen disrespects the husband and one who, like a thief steals even small things. (This type of wife) revere as a family diety one who is kind like a sister, one who is dear like a mother and one who is subject to you like a servant;[60]

(3) Abandon these six vices which result in loss of fame and birth in evil states. (a) Gambling (b) participation in festivals (c) laziness (d) association with sinful friends (e) drinking alcohol and (f) walking in the night.[61]

The Ratnāvalī[62] which is known as Rājaparikathā (translated into English) also is addressed probably to the same king giving some pieces of advice. Nāgārjuna conceives in it a state which almost resembles a welfare state. He prescribes the qualifications of a minister;[63]

Nītijñān dhārmikān snigdhāñ ।
śucīn bhaktān akātarān ।।
kulīnāñ śīlasaṁpannān ।
kṛtajñān sacivān kuru ।।

Prisoners must be properly taken care of.[64]

Yāvac ca na vimucyeraṃs ।
tāvat syuḥ sukhabandhanāḥ ।।
nāpita snāna pānānna ।
bhaiṣajya vasanān vitāḥ ।।

The poor, destitute and disabled must be provided with food and necessities of life.[65]

Andhavyādhita hīnāṅga ।
dīnānātha vanīpakāḥ ।।
te'py annapānaṃ sāmyena ।
labherann avighaṭṭitāḥ ।।

Compassion must be shown even to those who have committed grave sins. Punishment must be for reformation.[66]

tīvrapāpeṣu hiṁsreṣu ।
kṛpā kāryā viśeṣataḥ ।।
ta eva hi kṛpāpātraṁ ।
hatātmāno mahātmanām ।।

DEVELOPMENT OF PHILOSOPHY & LOGIC

As already noted in chapter three during the period of transition from Mahāsāṅghika system to Mahāyāna large quantities of Sūtra literature were produced in the Vihāras of Kṛṣṇā valley preserved by local Nāga race till Ācārya Nāgārjuna arrived on the scene. Ācārya Nāgārjuna systematised the Mahāyāna on the basis of the Prajñā Pāramitā literature. Mahāyāna branched off into Mādhyamaka and Yogācara while there developed Prāsaṅgika and Svātantrika sects among the Mādhyamikas. The philosophy of Nāgārjuna, the core of which was Sūnyavāda has been according to some scholars the source of inspiration for the development of Mayāvāda of Advaita of Śankarācārya.[67]

Incidentally, the exponents of the Mahāyāna systems found it neccessary to develop the science of logic in order to meet the criticism of their opponents and establish the superiority of Mahāyāna. The dialectical system of Nāgārjuna as elaborated in his Vigrahavyāvartanī may be said to be the first attempt in this direction. He declared that no one can find fault with the Mādhyamika system[68] and his dialectic was directed against the dogmatists and the rationalists.[69] Following him, *Dignāga* who adopted the Yogācara system occupies a pre-eminent place in the development of Indian logic.[70] He is rightly called the "Father of Indian Logic". Dharmakīrti surpassed even *Dignāga* in logic and even his worst critics acknowledge the intellectual eminence of Dharmakīrti as a logician.[71] In fact the contribution of *Dignāga* and Dharmakīrti was greater to the development of logic than to the growth of the Mahāyāna relgious system. Stcherbatsky rightly regards Dharmkīrti as "The Kant of India".[72]

LEARNING CENTRES IN ĀNDHRADEŚA

It has been noted above that the Āndhra Buddhist Vihāras witnessed from the beginning profound intellectual and literary activity. As a result Dhānyakaṭaka and Srīparvata developed into great educational centres in India. According to Gaṇḍavyūha, Dhānyakaṭaka was the most important centre of Bodhisattva doctrine.[73] Yuan Chwang records that at *Tena-ka-che-ka* the Saṅghārāmas are numerous, all study the law of the great vehicle.[74] He himself as studied the Abhidhamma at Dhānyakaṭaka.[75] To attract the attention of the mettle of Yuan chwang

Dhānyakaṭaka must have been a place of considerable reputation as an advanced Mahāyāna study centre. Lama Tārānātha, the Tibetan historian wrote that the great monastery near Lhasa with 7, 700 monks and a university with 6 colleges was built after the model of a monastery at Dhānyakaṭaka, the Mount Casino of the Deccan in the early centuries.[76]

Nāgārjunakoṇḍa also developed into a great centre of learning. Udyotana Sūri of the 8th century A.D. in his Prakrit work the Kuvalayamālā describes an educational institution called Mahāntaṁ maṭhaṁ[77] at Vijayapuri, which attracted students from Karṇākaraṇa, Mahārāshṭra, Lāṭa, Saurāṣṭra, Māḷava, Śrikaṇṭha and Sindh. The courses taught comprised Vyākaraṇa, Buddhist Sūtras, Sānkhya, Nyāya, Anekānta or Jaina and Lokāyata or Cārvāka philosophy. In this institution all were serious students with a few exceptions.

Though Vijayapuri did not exist till the 8th century A.D., Udyotana Sūri might have based his account of the great vihāra on the traditional account handed down from generation to generation. This only shows how the memory of Śrīparvata vihāra as a centre of learning was cherished till the time of Udyotana Sūri.

IMPACT OF MAHĀYĀNA ON ART

Mahāyānism freed the Artist from the fetters of traditional orthodoxy of representing the Bodhisattva or Buddha by symbols and inspired his creative impulse. The earlier spirit of Monastic resignation from worldly existence was replaced by love for life which began to pervade the whole world of art produced during this period.

Douglas Barret remarks[78] that the sudden outburst of creative activity in Āndhradeśa during 2nd century A.D. is naturally attributed to the inspiration of Mahāyānism.

The Buddha image carved at Amarāvati is not to express the abstract thought of the philosopher or logician but to satisfy the personal adoration or bhakti of the common laity and the simple monk, a need being displayed by the other contemporary religions. Debala Mitra remarks that during "the period of the rise of Mahāyāna, the art of the sculptors of Dhānyakaṭaka reached its zenith. Intoxicated with a creative impulse, they went on producing reliefs after reliefs which are now world famous for their superb expressions and exuberence of beauty."[79] The doctrinal changes were inevitably effected by the content of art and architecture. In the beginning, the focus was on the career of Śākyamuni which later shifted to the image of Buddha, bodhisattvas and the paradises. Therefore Buddha image began to occupy' the central position in relation to the stupa. The entire world of art underwent a great change with the introduction of the Buddha image.

Smith remarks[80] that Ferguson was of the opinion that the Amarāvati school "marked the culmination of the art of sculpture in India." He is prepared to agree with Havell that Amarāvati marbles offer delightful studies of animal life combined with extremely beautiful conventional ornaments" and that "The most varied and difficult movements of the human figure are drawn and modelled with great freedom and skill. The stiffness found in the earlier sculpture gave place to a movement.

Niharanjan Roy[81] rightly remarks that the Buddhas and Bodhisattvas represent the plastic process and find achievement of a highly subtle and mystical fluid and luminous thought known to us as the Mahāyāna - Yogācāra brought uptodate by contemporary Buddhist thinkers. They are the culmination of a spiritual quest. The plastic art represents the thought of Nāgārjuna. With the influence of Mahāyāna the art of Amaravati school reached to the highest level. Ānanda Coomaraswamy finds voluptuous beauty in the Nāgārjunakoṇḍa sculptures. This eroticism may be due to the influence of the Vaitulyaka ideas.[82]

IMPACT ON RELIGION

The development of Mahāyāna brought about remarkable changes in the religious life of the people. The Buddhist ideal of attadīpa and attasaraṇa was replaced by belief that one would attain Nirvāṇa by the grace of Buddha or Bodhisattva. Self effort was replaced by faith and discipline was replaced by devotion.

Buddha Bhakti is based on the idea that the virtue and power of an enlightened one are not confined to him but reach out to all, because of his devine power engendered by his transcendental wisdom and boundless compassion. In this form of Mahāyāna it is not the Buddha's teaching, but his life, personality and transcendental spiritual power and faith in him occupy the central place.

Mahāyāna as stated above laid more emphasis on Bhakti as a fundamental religious principle and so evolved an elaborated ritualism of worship of Buddhas and future Buddhas of high rank with dependance upon their grace. Faith developed in the grace of Buddhas and Bodhisattvas as gods who would fulfil their wishes, worship is efficacious in bringing happiness and ultimately the

Nirvāna. Then the images of Buddha were installed in Caityagṛhas and at cardinal points of stupas and viharas. Several images of Buddha in the round have been recovered from Amarāvatī, [83] Nāgārjunakoṇḍa and other Buddhist Kṣetras. One of the standing image of Nāgārjunakoṇḍa has a hole between its feet from which pearls, pieces of gold and other precious objects have been recovered.[84] It suggests that there was developed the ritual of consecrating the Buddha image. The images thus consecrated appear to have been decorated with jewels.The Amarāvatī inscription[85] of the Pallava king Simhavarman, who visited the Buddhakṣetra about 550 A.D. speaks of jewels wonderfully worked in gems, gold and silver (maṇi, kanaka, rajata, vichitra) flowers, lamps and sandal paste and incense were used in the worship and there was Nitya Naivedya. The Tummalaguḍem inscription[86] of Govindavarman of the 6th century A.D. records a gift to the vihāra for providing dīpa, dhūpa, gandha, puṣpa, pāna, bhojana, etc. which constitute aṅgabhoga. Mantras and Dhāraṇīs occupied a prominent place in the system of Mahāyāna worship. The worship by illumination is also recommended in the Śiksāsamuccaya Sūtra. Fa-hien noted that students of the Mahāyāna present offerings to the Prajñā Pāramitā and to Mañjuśrī.[87]

In the vihāras of Āndhra festivals like Vaiśākha Pūrṇimā were celebrated. An inscription from Nāgārjuna-koṇḍa describes a certain upāsaka Candraśrī[88] as the bestower of many religious gifts in connection with the celebration of religious ceremonies and festivals in honour of the Buddha, Dharma and Saṅgha. In his Ratnāvalī, Nāgārjuna appeals to the local ruler to allow and undisturb the functions such as Dēvadrōna[89] to continue. It may be assumed that on festive occasions images of Buddha were taken in procession in the streets of the neighbouring villages and towns. At several Buddhist places, bronze images[90] of Buddha have been discovered. They were probably used by the chief abbot of the place for his private worship. Further they were also used as Utsava Vigrahas. I-tsing advocates[91] the worship of Buddha with zeal and those who constantly offer incense and flowers to it are enabled to purify their thoughts and those who perpetually bath the image are enabled to ride over their sins. These developments had a twofold influence on religious history of the land. On one side it led to the emergence of Vajrayāna, for which also Āndhradeśa is considered as the birth place by many scholars.[92] Yuan Chwang wrote that in the caves very near to Dhānyakaṭaka, Vajrayāna Dhāraṇīs were produced[93] and the Tantrayāna work *Śekoddeśaṭīka* says that the Kālacakra Tantra was actually preached by the Buddha at Dhānyakaṭaka.[94] There is also a strong tradition that Dhānyakaṭaka came to be called Dhāraṇikōṭa because Daśabala (Buddha) deposited Dhāranīs at the place.[95] Dhānyakaṭaka[96] and Śālihuṇḍam[97] yielded several images of Vajrayāna gods and goddesses like Tārā, Mārici, Heruka and others.

On the other hand, Bhakti which was common to both Mahāyānism and Bhāgavatism served as a bridge between Buddhism and Brāhmanism. Already efforts were made to identify Buddha with the highest gods in the Hindu Pantheon. The Lalitavistara of the Mahāyānists[98] actually called the Buddha as Nārāyaṇa, Mahānārāyaṇa and Mahāpuruṣa. It was the culmination of the process that Buddha was admitted into the pantheon of Hindu gods as an incarnation of Nārāyaṇa. The Brahmanists also were inclined to worship Buddha, probably as an Avatāra of

Viṣṇu. The Ānandagotra king Damodaravarman was a Brahmanist but called himself the devotee of Samyaksaṁbuddha.[99] The Sālankāyana king Nandivarman-II (A.D. 450) was a Paramabhāgavata[100] but he made a gift to Mahāvihāra at Guṇṭupalli, out of veneration to Buddha.[101] Viṣṇukuṇḍins described themselves as the devotees of the Lord of Śrīparvata in their records. Śrīparvata is no other than Śrīparvata-Nāgārjunakoṇḍa. It is a well-known Buddhist kṣetra.[102] But from the records of the dynasty, we learn that the Viṣṇukuṇḍins were Brahmanists with leanings to Vaiṣṇavism. Govindavarman compares himself with Lord Govinda where as his son Mādhavavarman was compared to Keśava. Therefore it is reasonable to hold that the Viṣṇukuṇḍins were the devotees of Śrīparvataswāmy, the Buddha as an incarnation of Viṣṇu. About the same time, that is 5th and 6th centuries A.D. the Guptas in the north also followed Vaiṣṇavism.[103] Buddha had already become an incarnation of Viṣṇu. These developments in the north should have influenced the Viṣṇukuṇḍins and thay too made Śrīparvataswāmy as their family god.[104]

Thus the Buddha gradually came to be identified with Viṣṇu. There is an interesting Navāvatāra panel[105] in the temple of sūrya at Alampur (Mahaboobnagar Dt.). Thus Buddha is given in the panel the central position and his image is slightly bigger than those of the other Avatāras that surround him. The panel gives the impression that the Buddha was conceived as Mahāpuruṣa and that the Avatāras emanate from him. The identification of the Buddha and Viṣṇu was thus complete.

RESUME

Buddhism became popular in Āndhra even before

Aśoka convened the Third Saṅgiti. The Andhakas or the Āndhra Buddhist monks appear to have been in the forefront of all the developments in the Buddhist thought and practice, right from the beginning.

The Andhakas who were also known as the Caityakas might have supported the break-up of the Saṅgha into Theravāda and Mahāsāṅghika schools in the second Saṅgīti. From that time, Āndhradēśa became the strong hold of the Mahāsāṅghikas.

After the death of Aśoka, during the times when Brahmanism was reformed and revived, the Mahāsāṅghikas felt deeply concerned for the future of the Buddha Dharma. With the support of the Upāsakas of the rich merchant and artisan classes, the Mahāsāṅghikas brought out the deeper and intricate teaching of the Buddha in the form of the elaborate sūtras or the Vaipulya sūtras. There are plenty of literary and archaeological epigraphical and sculptural evidecne in support of the view that the Vaipulya sūtras were produced in the Caityaka Vihāras of the Kṛṣṇā valley.

Basing on the sūtras, especially Prajñāpāramitā, Ācārya Nāgārjuna systematised the new trends in Buddhism into Mahāyāna and based it on Mādhyamika philosophy whose cardinal principle is Śūnyatā. His successors, Āryadēva, Buddhapālita and Bhāvaviveka developed the Mādhyamika system but in the hands of last two it broke up into Prāsaṅgika and Svatantrika schools.

In Mahāyāna there developed another school known as the Yogācāra or Vijñānavāda at the hands of Maitreyanātha, Asaṅga and Vasubandhu, who were not associated with Āndhra. But two of its greatest exponents, Dignāga and Dharmakīrti lived in Āndhra. They logically defended Yogācāra and preached it.

The rise and development of Mahāyāna had a profound impact on the social, economic and cultural life of Āndhradeśa. As it did not lay emphasis on monastic life. large number of men and women accepted Buddhism and promoted its cause. Socially, Mahāyānism produced among people a cosmopolitan spirit and a selfless concern for the welfare of mankind. The permission given by Mahāyāna to the enjoyment of worldly pleasures within the fold of Dharma gave stimulus to economic activity in the land and it may be said that the period from 1st century B.C. to 3rd century A.D. is the most prosperous period in the economic history of Āndhradeśa.

It has been noted that large quantities of Sūtra and Śāstra literature of very high philosophical order was produced during this period. The rich contribution made by *Dignāga* and Dharmakīrti to the system of Indian logic is unsurpassed. The love of life preached by Mahāyāna revolutionised the Āndhra school of art which could produce some of the best specimens of Indian art by any standard. Dhānyakaṭaka and Śrīparvata became great centres of higher learning whose memory had been cherished for centuries.

In the field of religion, Mahāyāna gradually led to the rise of Vajrayāna. On the other side, devotionalism brought Buddhism and neo-Brahmanism closer and the Buddha was incorporated into Hinduism as the 9th Avatāra of Viṣṇu. These developments are alleged to have been the cause for the decline of Buddhism in general.

REFERENCES

1. T.N. Ramachandran, *Nāgapattanam and other Bronze images in the Madras Govt. Museum*, pp. 59-60.
2. Burgess. *Notes on the Amarāvati Stūpa*, (Madras, 1882), p. 54.

3. *Ibid*, p. 41.
4. *Ibid*, p. 41.
5. R. Subrahmanyam, *śālihundam the Buddhist site in Āndhra pradesh*, (Hyderabad, 1964) p. 123.
6. *Ibid.*
7. Luders list no. 1202.
8. Burgess, op. cit, p. 18.
9. *Ibid*, p. 25.
10. I.K.Sarma, "Epigraphical discoveries at Guntupalli", Journal of Epigraphical Society, vol.v, p. 55.
11. Epigraphia Indica, vol.x, no.1336.
12. Chanda, Some unpublished Amarāvati inscriptions, E.I. XV 1919-20, (Calcutta, 1925), p. 264.
13. Burges op. cit. p. 30.
14. E.I. Vol. XX, Nāgārjunakoṇḍa inscriptions, No.F.
15. *Ibid*, Vol.XXXIII, p. 190.
16. *Ibid*, Vol.XX, Nāgārjunakoṇḍa, Inscription No.F.
17. *Ibid.*
18. Luders List, 1218.
19. E.I. Vol. XX, Nāgārjunakoṇḍa, Inscriptions No. J.
20. B.S.L.Hanumantharao, *Religion in Āndhra* (Guntur, 1973) p. 67.
21. E.I. Vol. XXXIII, pp. 147-149 and E.I. Vol.XXXIV, pp. 19-20.
22. *Ibid*, Vol.VIII, Nasik Inscription NO.2, p. 60 ff.
23. Select inscriptions, Vol.I, p. 169.
24. *Ibid*, Vol.VIII, Nasik, inscription, op. cit.
25. Burgess, Buddhist stūpas of Amaravati and Jaggayyapeṭa, p. 110.
26. E.I. Vol.XXXV, p. 13.
27. *Ibid*, vol.xx, Inscriptions of Nāgārjunakoṇḍa
28. K.A.N. Sastri (Ed.) *Comprehensive History of India*, Vol.II, p. 304.
29. Luders List No. 1303 and Burgress, *Notes on Amarāvati Stupas*, p. 64.
30. P.V.Kane, *History of Dharmaśāstra*, Vol.V, Part-II, (Poona, 1958), p. 926.
31. E.I. vol.XX, Nāgārjunakoṇḍa inscriptions, B5.
32. *Ibid*, No.F.
33. Burgress, *Buddhist Stūpas of Amarāvati and Jaggayyapeta.* (London, 18870 pl.XI, fig.2.
34. Burgress, *Notes on Amarāvati Stūpa*, p. 30.

35. *Ibid*, p. 41.
36. Edward Conze, *Buddhist Meditation* (London, 1956), p. 176.
38. B.S.L.Hanumantha Rao, *Age of the Sātavāhanas*, (Hyderabad, 1976), p. 44.
39. E.I. Vol.XX, Nāgārjunakoṇḍa inscriptions, No.F.
40. *Ibid*, No.C3.
41. M.A.S.I., No.71, pl.XB.
42. E.I., Vol.XX, No.F. p. 22.
43. *Ibid*, vol.XXXV, p. 18.
44. *Ibid*, Vol.XXXV, p. 8.
45. Ramachandran Jain, (ed.) *Mc. Crindle, Ancient India as described by Ptolemy* by (Delhi, 1975), p. 68.
46. Burgess, Buddhist Stūpas of Amarāvati and Jaggayyapeta, pp. 72-85.
47. I.K. Sarma, "Epigraphical Discoveries at Guṇṭupalli", *Journal of Epigraphical Society of India*, (1978), Vol.V, p. 49.
48. *Epigraphia Āndhrica*, Vol.II, p. 112.
49. *Epigraphia Indica*, Vol.XXXIII, pp. 189-191 ff.
50. H.Sicar, Presidential Address to Āndhra Pradesh History Congress (1986, Guntur), pp. 14-16.
51. Mc. Crindle, op. cit.
52. M.A.S.I., No.54, p. 6.
53. Sukumar Dutt, *Buddhism in East Asia*, (Delhi, 1966), pp. 52-58.
54. P.N. Chopra, (Ed.) *Buddhism in India and abroad*, (Delhi, 1980), pp. 35-38.
55. Edward Conze, *The Prajñā Pāramitā Literature*, p. 9.
56. K.Satchidananda Murty, Āndhra Contribution to Buddhist Thought, (Dr. S. Radhakrishnan Memorial Lecture) (Hyderabad, 1980), p. 15.
57. M. Winternitz, *History of Indian Literature*, Vol.II. (Delhi, 1977), p. 344.
58. Ven Lozong James Pal and Ven Agawang Samta Choppel, Peter Della Santina, *Nāgārjuna's letter to King Gautamīputra*, (Delhi, 1983, reprint).
59. *Ibid*-38.
60. *Ibid*-36.
61. *Ibid*-37.

62. Michael Hahn, *Nāgārjuna's Ratnāvalī,* Vol.I, The Basic Texts, (Bonn 1982).
63. Ratnāvalī IV, 23.
64. *Ibid*-35.
65. *Ibid*-20.
66. *Ibid* - 32.
67. Sir Charles Eliot, *Hinduism and Buddhism,* Vol.II, pp. 74-75.
68. Jaydev Singh, *An Introduction to Mādhyamika Philosophy,* (Delhi, 1978), p. 17.
69. *Ibid.*
70. N.Dutt, In the *Classical Age*, p. 387. (Bombay, 1980)
71. Buston Vol.II, p. 154.
72. Debi Prasad Chattopadhyaya (Ed.), *Studies in the History of Indian Philosophy*, (Calcutta, 1979), Vol.III, p. 265.
73. N.Dutt, Preface to Buddhism in Orissa, p. iv.
74. S.Beal, *Buddhist Records of the Western World*, (Delhi, 1983), Vol.II, p. 221.
75. T. Watters, *On Yuan chwang's Travels in India,* Vol.II, p. 217.
76. Inidan Antiquary, Vol.IV, p. 363.
77. G.S.Dikshit, Proceedings of the Āndhra Pradesh History Congress, Presidential Address (Kakinada, 1983)
78. Douglas Barret, *Sculptures from Amarāvati in British Museum,* (London, 1954), p. 59, p1.-11.
79. Debala Mitra, *Buddhist Monuments,* (Calcutta, 1971), p. 200.
80. P.V. Bapat, "Contribution of Buddhism to Indian Culture, " in *Buddhism in India and Abroad*, (P. N.Chopra (Ed.), (Delhi, 1980), p. 33.
81. Niharanjan Ray in *Classical Age*, p. 540.
82. A.K.Coomaraswamy, *History of Indian and Indonesian Art* (London, 1927).
83. M.L.Nigam, *Sculptural Art of Āndhra*, (Delhi, 1980), pp. 36-37.
84. M.A.S.I., No.71, pl.XIV, A&B.
85. Burgess, *Notes on Amarāvati Stūpa*, (Madras, 1882), p. 49.
86. *Bhārati*, Telgu Monthly, July, 1965- Indra Pālanagara plates-line 22.
87. Oldenberg - Introduction to *Vinayapitaka*, Vol.I, p. XL ii.
88. E.I. Vol.XXXIV, p. 273.
89. Journal of Royal Asiatic Society, 1934, pp. 308-325.

90. T.N.Ramachandran, *"Nāgapattanam and other Bronzes" in the Madras Government Museum Bulletin*, pp. 59-60.
91. Haripada Chakraborti, *Asceticism in Ancient India Brāhmanical, Buddhist and Jain* (Calcutta, 1973), p. 314.
92. L.M.Joshi, "Original Home of Tāntric Buddhism". *Journal of Oriental Institute*, Vol.XVI. pp. 223-232.
93. T.Watters. *On Yuan Chwang's Travels in India*, Vol.II, p. 215.
94. Sir Charles Eliot, *Hinduism and Buddhism*, Vol.II, p. 386.
95. L.M.Joshi, op. cit.
96. B.S.L.Hanumantha Rao, *Religion in Āndhra*, p. 122.
97. B.Bhattacharya, *The Indian Buddhist Iconography*, (Calcutta, 1958), p. 221.
98. Lefmann (Ed.) *Lalitavistara* (Halle, 1902), Ch, XV, pp. 202 and 229.
99. E.I., Vol.XVII, pp. 327-330.
100. "Pedavegi plates", *Journal of Āndhra Historical Research Society*, I, pp. 92-102. According to his Pedavegi plates he made gifts to Viṣṇugṛha swāmy which clearly indicates that he was Vaiṣṇavite by faith even the Guṇṭupalli inscription calls him a Parama bhāgavata.
101. *Bharati* (Telugu monthly), 1978, pp. 28-29.
102. Tummalagudem Records, *Epigraphia Āndhrica*, Vol.II, pp. 9-11.
103. Radhakumud Mookerji, *The Gupta Empire* (Delhi, 1973), 5th edition, pp. 130-131.
104. *Bharati*, July 1965, Indrapalanagara plates of Vikramendravarman, pp. 14-131.
105. B.S.L.Hanumantha Rao, "Śrīparvataswāmy of Viṣṇukundins", *Journal of Indian History*, (Trivandram), Vol.XL, pp. 49-60.

BIBLIOGRAPHY

PRIMARY SOURCES

Literary:

Amarakośa, Amarasimha, Nirnaya Sagara Press, (Bombay, 1911.)

Āpastamba Sūtras, (tr.) by Buhler, Sacred Books of the East, Vol.II (London, 1932).

Aṣṭasāhasrikā Prajñā Pāramitā, (tr.) Edward Conze (Calcutta, 1958).

Bhagavadgītā, (Ed.) S.Radhakrishnan (London, 1948).

Bhagavadgītā, (Ed.) A.D.Hill, (London, 1928).

Buddha Carita of Aśvaghoṣa, E. H.Johnston (Ed.), (Delhi, 1978).

Buddhist Texts through the ages, (Ed.), Edward Conze, I.B.Horner, David Snellgrove, and Arthur Waley, (New York, 1954).

The Cullavagga, Sacred Books of the East (Vol. XVII and XX (ed.), O Idenberg (Delhi, 1981).

Dhammapada, Hultzch, P.T.S. (London, 1906-15).

Dīpavaṁśa, H.Oldenberg, (New Delhi, 1982), reprint.

Dvādaśa Nikāya Śāstra, Richard Robinson (Holland, 1982).

Gāthāsaptaśati, Nirnayasagar Press, (Bombay, 1969).

Katha-Vatthu from the Abhidhamma pitaka, Points of Controversy, shwe zan Aung and Mrs. Rhys Davids P.T.S. London 1960.

Kathāsaritsāgara, Nirnayasagar Press, (Bombay, 1915).

Lalitavistara, (Ed.), Lefmann, (Halle, 1902).

Nāgārjuna's Letter to King Gautamīputra, Ven. Lozong James Pal, Ven. Agawang Samta Choppel and Peter Della Santina, (Delhi, 1983), (reprint).

Ratnāvalī, Giuseppe Tucci, J.R.A.S. 1934 & 1936.

Ratnavalī, Michael Hann (Ed.), (Bonn, 1982).

Saddharma Puṇḍarīka sūtra, H.Kern & B.Nanjio (Ed.), (St. Petersburg, 1912).

Śikṣā samuccaya of Śāntideva, (Ed.) C.Bendall. (St.Petersburg, 1897-1902).

A Study of Mahāvastu, B.C.Law, (Delhi, 1978).

Suttanipāta, F. Max Müller (tr.), Sacred Book of the East, Vol.X, part-II (Delhi, 1968).

The Largest Sūtra on Perfect Wisdom, Edward Conze, (Delhi, 1979).

The Holy Teaching of Vimalakīrti, Robert A.F. Thurman (tr.), (London, 1976).

Vigrahavyāvartanī, (Telugu), G.V.Krishna Rao, (Tenali, 1964).

ARCHAEOLOGICAL SOURCES

Amarāvati Sculptures in Madras Government Museum, C.Śivarāma Murty, (Madras. 1977).

Ancient India, No.16.

Annual Report of Archaeological Survey of India, Southern Circle, 1916-17, Alexander Rea.

Buddhist Stūpas of Amarāvati and Jaggayyapeṭa, Burgess Jas, (London, 1887).

Corpus Inscriptionum Indicarum, (Delhi, 1969).

Epigraphia Āndhrica, Vol.I & II.

Epigraphia Carnatica, Vol.VII.

Epigraphia Indica, Vol.VIII, X, XV, XX, XXIV, XXVII, XXXV, XXXVI, XXXVIII.

Indian Antiquary, Vol.IV, V, IX.

Memoirs of Archaeological Survey of India, No. 54, A.H.Longhurst.

Memoirs of Archaeological Survey of India, No.71, T.N.Ramachandran.

Nāgapattinam and other Bronzes in the Madras Government Museum. T.N. Ramachandran. (Madras Govt. Museum Bulletin, 1965).

Notes on Amarāvati Stūpa, Burgess Jas, (Madras, 1882).

SECONDARY SOURCES

Modern works

Alchin, Birth of Indian Civilization (Panvil Series, 1968).

Alexander Cunningham, The Ancient Geography of India, (Delhi, 1975).

Bapat, P.V. (Ed.), 2500 years of Buddhism, (Delhi, 1956).

Basham, A.L., History and Doctrines of the Ajivikas, A Vanquished Indian Religion, (London, 1951).

Beal, S., (tr.) Shaman-Hwui Li, Life of Hiuen-Tsang, (Delhi, 1973). (2nd.Ed).

Beal, S. (tr.) Buddhist Records of the Western World, (Delhi, 1983).

Benjamin Rowland, The Evolution of Buddha Image, (New York, 1976).

Bhandarkar R.G., Vaiṣṇavism, Śaivism and Minor Religious systems (Poona, 1928).

Chopra P.N. (Ed.) Buddhism in India and Abroad (Delhi, 1980).

Conze Edward, Buddhist Thought in India, (London, 1962).

Conze Edward, Buddhist Meditation (London, 1956).

Conze Edward, A Short History of Buddhism (London, 1981).

Conze Edward, Thirty Years of Buddhist Studies (London, 1967).

Coomaraswamy A.K. Yakshas (Washington, 1928).

Coomaraswamy A.K. Origin of the Buddha Image (New Delhi, 1980).

Coomaraswamy A.K. History of the Indian and Indonesian Art (London, 1927).

Daisaku Ikeda, Buddhism in the first millennium (Tokyo, 1977).

Debi Prasad Chattopadhyaya (Ed.) Studies in the History of Indian Philosophy, Vol.III (Calcutta, 1979).

Debi Prasad Chattopadhyaya (Ed.) Taranatha's History of Buddhism in India (Calcutta, 1980).

Debala Mitra, Buddhist Monuments (Calcutta, 1971).

Douglas Barret, Sculptures from Amarāvati in British Museum (London, 1954).

Dube S.N. Cross Currents in early Buddhism (Delhi, 1980).

Dutt Nalinaksha, Mahāyāna Buddhism (Delhi, 1976).

Dutt Nalinaksha, Buddhist Sects in India (Delhi, 1978).

Dutt Nalinaksha, Aspects of Mahāyāna Buddhism and its relation to Hīnayāna (London, 1930).

Dutt Sukumar, Buddhist Monks and Monasteries of India (London, 1962).

Dutt Sukumar, Buddhism in East Asia (Delhi, 1966).

Eliot, Sir Charles, Hinduism and Buddhism, Vol.I, II, & III (London, 1957).

Foucher A., Beginnings of Buddhist Art and other Essays on Indian and Central Asian Archaeology, (Eng. tr.) by L.A.Thomas and F.W.Thomas (London, 1914).

Gopalachari K. Early History of the Āndhra Country, (2nd Ed.) (Madras, 1976).

Goyal S.R. Religious History of Ancient India, Vol. I&II (Meerut, 1984).

George N. Roerich, Blue Annals, (reprint) (Delhi, 1979).

Gururaja Rao, B.K. Megalithic Culture in South India. (Mysore 1972)

Hanumantha Rao B.S.L. Religion in Āndhra (Guntur, 1973).

Hanumantha Rao B.S.L. The Age of Sātavāhanas (Hyderabad, 1978).

Hardayal, The Bodhisattva Doctrine in Buddhist Sanskrit Literature (Delhi, 1978).

Haripada Chakraborthi, Asceticism in Ancient India, Brāhmanical, Buddhist and Jain (Calcutta, 1973).

Hopkin. The Religions in India (Boston, 1895).

Jacobi H, Studies in Jainism (Ahmedabad, 1946).

Jaydev Singh, An Introduction to Mādhyamika Philosophy (Delhi, 1978).

Jaiswal S. The Origin and development of Vaiṣṇavism (Delhi, 1967).

Joshi L.M. Studies in the Buddhistic Culture of India (Delhi, 1967).

Keith A.B. Buddhist Philosophy in India and Ceylon (Oxford, 1923).

Kern H. Manual of Indian Buddhism, 2nd Ed. (Delhi, 1972).

Kimura Ryukan, A Historical Study of the terms Hīnayana and Mahāyāna and the origin of Mahāyāna Buddhism. (Delhi 1978).

Krishna Rao B.V. History of the Early Dynasties of Āndhradeśa (Madras, 1942).

Majumdar R.C. History and Culture of the Indian People. Vol.II (Age of Imperial Unity) and Vol.III (Classical Age).

Mc Crindle, Ancient India as described by Ptolemy (Calcutta, 1927).

Mc Crindle, The Ancient Geography of India (Delhi, 1975).

Mukharji R.K. Aśoka (Delhi, 1972), (reprint).

Mukharji R.K. The Gupta Empire (Delhi, 1973).

Murty T.R.V. The Central Philosophy of Buddhism (London, 1980).

Narayana Aiyar C.V. Śaivism in South India (Madras 1936).

Nigam M.L. Sculptural Art of Āndhradeśa (Delhi, 1980).

Niharanjan Ray, Mauryan and Post Mauryan Art (Delhi, 1975).

Obermiller (tr.) Buston's History of Buddhism Vol. I & II (Hiedelburg, 1932).

Pandey G.C. Studies in the Origins of Buddhism, (Delhi, 1974).

Pandey R.C. Buddhist Studies in India (Delhi, 1975).

Ramachandra Rao P.R. The Art of Nāgārjunakoṇḍa (Madras, 1956).

Ramanan K.V. Nāgārjuna's Philosophy (Delhi, 1978).

Ramanan M. Sātavāhana Commemoration Volume (Guntur, 1946).

Randle H.N. Fragments from Dignāga (Delhi, 1981).

Richard Robinson, Early Mādhyamika in India and China (Delhi, 1976).

Sangharakshita (Ed.) Eternal Legacy (London, 1985).

Satchidananda Murty K. Nāgārjuna (Delhi, 1983).

Satchidananda Murty K. Āndhra Contribution to Buddhist Thought (1980).

Amala Prajna Prof. N.H. Samtani & H.S. Prasad (ed.) Aspects of Buddhist Studies, P.V. Bapat Felicitation Volume. (Indian Book Centre, Delhi).

Sastri A.M. Outlines of Early Buddhism (Banaras, 1965).

Sastri K.A.N. History of South India (London, 1958).

Sastri K.A.N. Foreign Notices of South India (Madras, 1939).

Sastri K.A.N. (Ed.) The Age of the Nandas and Mauryas (Delhi, 1967).

Sastri K.A.N. (Ed.) Comprehensive History of India, Vol.II.

Smith V.A. The Oxford History India. (Oxford 1958)

Subrahmanyam K.R. Buddhist Remains in Āndhra and the History of South India between 225-610 A.D. (Waltair, 1932).

Subrahmanyam R. Śālihuṇḍam (Hyderabad, 1964).

Suzuki D.T. Outlines of Mahāyāna Buddhism (London, 1907).

Suzuki B.L. Mahāyāna Buddhism (London, 1981).

Stcherbatsky, Buddhist Logic, Vol.I (Hague, 1958).

Thomas E.J. The History of Buddhist Thought (London, 1963).

Vogel J. Ph. Indian Serpent Lore (London, 1926).

Vogel J. Ph. Buddhist Art in India, Ceylon and Java (Delhi, 1977). (English translation).

Warder A.K. Indian Buddhism (Delhi, 1970).

Watters T. On Yuan Chwang's Travels in India (Delhi, 1973), Vol. I &II.

Webers, History of Indian Literature (London, 1914).

Winternitz M. History of Indian Literature, Vol.II (Delhi, 1977).

Yazdani G. Early History of the Deccan, 2 volumes (Hyderabad. 1960).

PERIODICALS AND OTHER SOURCES

1. Ancient India, Vol. 16, 1967.
2. Bhārati - (Telugu Monthly), 1956, 1978, 1987.
3. Encyclopaedia of Religion and Ethics, Vols. II, IV, V, VI andVIII.
4. Encyclopaedia of Buddhism - Vols. I and II.
5. Indian Antiquary, Vols. IV and X.
6. Indian Archaeology - A Review.
7. Indian Historical Quarterly, Vols. III, VII, XXXI, XXXII.

8. Journal of Indian History, Trivendrum, Vol. XL.

9. Journal of Āndhra Historical Research Society, Vols, I, XXVI.

10. Journal of Epigraphical Society of India, Vols, V, IX.

11. Journal of Royal Asiatic Society, 1910, 1934, 1936, 1947.

12. Journal of Asiatic Society of Bengal, 1937.

13. Journal of Oriental Institute, Vol. XVI.

14. Śatavāhana Commemoration Volume, 1946, Guntur.

15. Śatavāhana Sañcika, 1946, Guntur.

16. Story of Buddhism with Special Reference to South India. (Aiyappan A. and Śrīnivasan P.R., published by the Government of Madras, Department of information and publicity 1960). In Commemoration of the 2500th Buddha Jayanti Celebration at the Madras Museum, 1956.

INDEX

Abhayagiri, 45
Abhidhamma, 43, 109
Abhimukhi, 45
Abhisamayālaṃkārāloka, 88
Acala, 15
Ācharya Nāgārjuna, 7, 18, 55, 65, 66, 92, 108, 116
Ādāpur, 35
Adhammikas, 5
Ādi Buddha, 11, 12, 50
Advaita, 108
Advayaṁ, 19, 31
Advayavādi, 16, 55, 65
Advēṣa, 28
Agapogalasa, 48
Ahiṁsa, 27
Ahhubuddhi, 100
Aiyaswamy sastry, 84, 85
Akṣara Śataka, 80
Akṣhobhya, 12
Akuthobhaya, 72
Ālaṁbana parikṣa, 87
Alampur, 115
Altruistic morality, 16
Amarakōsa, 16
Amarāvati, 33, 36, 37, 38, 43, 52, 55, 103, 110, 111, 112, 113
Amitābha, 11, 12, 71
Amitāyurdhyāna, 6
Amōghasiddhi, 12
Ānand Coomaraswamy, 112
Ānandagotras, 114
Anātma, 7, 9, 17, 18
Andhaka, 41, 46, 54, 55
Andhakavinda suttānta, 81
Anekanta, 110
Aṅga, 31, 32
Aṅgabhōga, 52
Animism, 30, 37
Aparaśaila, 43, 55
Āpastaṁba, 35, 38
Arcismati,15
Arhat naṅda, 31
Arhat, 42, 44, 46
Arhathood, 19, 41
Arhatyāna, 5
Ārjava, 27
Arthaśāstra, 30, 35
Āryadeva, 2, 4, 8, 77, 78, 79, 80, 81, 82, 92, 106, 116
Āryans, 29, 38, 40
Āryasaṅghaṁ, 42
Āryasūra, 90, 92
Asaṅga, 2, 9

Aśoka, 3, 28, 33, 34, 36, 115, 116
Aṣṭāṅgamārga, 19
Aṣṭāsāhasrika Prajñāpāramitā, 32, 55
Asvaghōṣa, 6, 7, 31, 68, 78,
Attadīpa, 45
Attaśaraṇa, 45
Avadāna, 14
Avalōkitēśwara, 13, 15, 75
Avataṁsaka, 6, 7, 54
Avenika dharmas, 49
Bala, 14
Banavāsi, 36
Barnett, 13
Besnagar, 40
Bhadaṅta Nāgārjuna, 68
Bhagavadgīta, 25, 27, 28,
Bhagavān, 47
Bhāgavatism, 3, 25, 27, 39, 101, 114
Bhakti, 15, 24, 25, 26, 28, 29, 38, 112
Bhattiprōlu, 35, 47, 51, 105
Bhāvavivēka, 2, 8, 65, 82, 83, 84, 85, 106, 116
Bhavya, 85
Bhikku, 17
Blue annals, 67
Bōdhan, 65
Bōdhi, 13
Bōdhicitta, 13
Bōdhisattva, 10, 11, 12, 13, 15, 17, 26, 31, 46, 49, 104
Bōdhisattvayāna, 5
Bodhisiri, 52
Brahma, 1, 50
Brahmanical, 78, 80, 104
Brāhmanism, 3, 26, 27, 34, 38, 39, 41
Brahmavihāras, 19
Brihatkatha, 77
Budhacarita, 7
Buddhahood, 10, 13, 19, 53
Buddhapālita, 2, 65, 82, 85
Buddharakkhita, 100
Buddhavacana, 9, 54
Buddhayāna, 7
Buhler, 35
Buston, 89, 90, 92
Caitya, 15, 16, 51
Caityagiri, 44
Caityaka, 43, 44, 46 55, 116
Caityaśaila, 43, 44
Caṁtisiri, 52, 102
Candraprabha, 68
Caṅdavaram, 35
Candragōmin, 90
Candrakīrti, 77, 78
Candraprabha, 68
Candrasri, 113
Cankisutta, 29
Cārvāka, 110
Catuh sataka, 79, 80, 82

Cetika, 43
Cetikiya, 43
Cetiyavādaka, 43
Cetiyavaṁdaka, 43
Ceylon, 45, 82
Chandōgya upanishad, 25
Chandragomin, 90
Chandrakīrti, 88
Chebrolu, 35
Chizen Akanuma, 10
Cittavisuddhi Prakaraṇa, 79, 81
Codana prakaraṇa, 91
Compassion, 8, 13, 15, 16, 17, 48, 112
Cūdāmaṇi, 89
Daisaku Ikeda, 4
Damodara Varma, 114
Dāna, 14, 27, 81
Daṅtapura, 82
Dasabalamahābala, 47
Daśabhūmika sūtra, 6
Daśabhūmisūtra, 15
Daśabhūmivibhāsa śastra, 72, 74
Daśavatthūni, 4
Debala mitra, 111
Dela Valle Poussin, 24, 26
Devadroṇa, 113
Devagiri, 103
Dēvarāja Sakatasa, 47
Dēvātidēva, 11, 47
Devotion, 15, 25, 26, 27,
Devotionalism, 11
Dhammapada, 27, 28, 29, 75
Dhammasaṅgani, 29
Dhānyakataka, 32, 33, 42, 43, 47, 51, 54, 71, 83, 105, 109, 111, 114, 117
Dharaṇikōta, 114
Dhāraṇis, 15, 114
Dharma śūnyata, 11, 18
Dharmachakra, 51
Dharmadhātu, 50, 55, 77
Dharmakāya, 12
Dharmakīrti, 65, 89, 90, 91, 92, 106, 116, 117
Dharmamēgha, 15
Dharmapāla, 83, 89, 90, 91
Dhātus, 49, 51
Dhātuvara, 50
Dhyāna, 14
Dhyāni Buddhas, 12
Dignāga, 65, 83, 86, 87, 88, 89, 92, 109, 116, 117
Dīpakarṇi, 78
Divinity of Buddha, 47
Dukkha, 9
Dūrangama, 15
Dusaka, 42
Dvādasanikāya Śāstra, 72, 75, 82
Dvēṣa, 28
Dviyāna, 15

Edward conze, 2
Ekayāna, 5
Esoteric, 2
Eśvarakrishṇa, 88
Eśvarasēna, 87
Exoteric, 2
Gāthāsaptaśati, 41
Gahapati, 3, 36
Gājulabaṇḍa, 35
Gaṇḍavyūha, 6, 32, 33, 54, 109
Gāndhāra, 24, 25 30
Ganges, 81
Garuḍa Pillar, 40
Gautamiputra śātakarṇi, 41, 101
Ghaṇṭasāla, 36, 105
Gōdāvari, 30
Goyal, 27
Grierson, 39
Guḍimallaṁ, 40
Guhyaupadēsa, 2
Guṇṭupalli, 36
Haghasiri, 100
Hala, 69
Harappa, 29
Harsha, 90
Haribhadra, 88
Hastavala Prakaraṇa, 79, 80
Havell, 111
Heruka, 114
Hetubindu, 91
Heliodorus, 40
Hētucakraḍamaru, 87
Hīnayāna, 4, 5, 7, 8, 9, 10, 11
Hiramutthuva, 103
Hugha, 100
Indo- Bactrians, 3, 40
Indra, 26
Indrapālanagara grant, 48
Isvarasēna, 89
Itsing, 26
Jaggayyapēta, 47, 53, 68
Jaina, 30
Jainism, 29
Jallundar, 26
Jātaka,14
Jatakamāla, 90, 92
Jayaprabha, 68
Jayavarman, 19
Jina, 30
Jinendrabuddhi 87
Jñāna, 14
Jñānasāra Samuccaya, 79
Jñeyāvaraṇa, 19
Juska, 69
Kalacakratantra, 114
Kaliṅga, 30, 36
Kaliṅgapatṇaṁ, 82
Kaṅchi, 36, 86
Kāne, 35
Kanishka, 6, 26, 30, 31, 68, 69
Kantakasela, 103
Kāpālika, 33
Karatālaratna, 84

Kārika, 72
Karma, 28
Karuṇā, 68
Kāsyapa, 13
Kathāsaritsāgara, 71
Kathāvatthu, 33, 45, 55
Kautilya, 30
Keith, 24, 26
Kern, 71
Kēsanapalli, 52
Khāravela, 30
Kimura, 7, 83
Klēśāvaraṇa, 18
Kōḍābalisiri, 5, 53
Konḍāpur, 35, 38
Kṛṣṇa, 39
Kṛṣṇavalley, 34, 36, 53, 55, 108
Kṣānti, 14
Ksatriya, 27
Kumārajiva, 69, 70, 77, 78, 81
Kumāranandi, 53
Kumārilabhatta, 88, 90
Kushana, 68
Kusumamāla, 6
Laity, 17
Lalitavistara, 13, 51, 114
Laṅkāvatārasūtra, 67
Lata, 110
Lhasa, 110
Liṅga, 40
Lōkōttara, 44
Lōgathikasa, 48
Lōkōttaravādins, 44, 54
Longhurst, 105
Mādhava, 90
Mādhyamaka Pratītyasamutpāda, 85
Mādhyamakārtha Saṁgraha, 84, 85
Mādhyamika, 65, 66, 75, 77, 81, 82, 85
Mādhyamaka hṛdaya vṛtti Tarka Jvāla, 84
Mādhyamka vṛtti, 82, 83
Madhyamikas, 108, 116
Madhyamaka Sastra, 82
Mādhyamakavatāra pradīpa, 85, 86
Magdian, 24
Mahābhāsya, 30
Mahacaitya, 103
Mahādeva, 4, 41, 42, 43, 45
Mahākaruṇa, 17
Mahāmatras, 35
Mahāmayasūtra, 67
Mahāmēghasūtra, 66
Mahānāga, 70
Mahanavikas, 105
Mahāpadmanaṅda, 30
Mahāparinibbānasutta, 15
Mahāpurusha, 114
Mahārāstra, 110
Mahāsāṅghika, 1, 2, 5, 31, 41, 42, 43, 53, 55, 116

Mahāśūnyatavādins, 45
Mahāvaṁsa, 37
Mahāvastu, 13, 44, 54
Mahāviharavāsins, 53
Mahāyāna viṁśaka, 85
Mahāyānakaratāla Ratṇa Śāstra, 84
Maisolia, 105
Maitreya, 15, 86
Maitreyanātha, 65, 75
Maitri, 28
Majjimanikāyadhara, 42
Mahākaruṇā, 17
Mahāvastu, 13, 44, 54
Mahavihāravāsins, 53
Malava, 110
Malayagiri, 83
Mañjuśrī, 15, 18, 31, 54, 75, 86,113
Mañjuśrīmūlakalpa, 18, 67
Mañjuśrīmūlataṅtra, 77
Mantras, 15
Marici, 114
Mathura, 25
Mahāvaṁsa, 37
Maurya, 3, 25, 33, 34
Maxmuller, 24, 26
Māyāvāda, 108
Megalithic, 37, 38
Mlecchas, 34
Mother goddesses, 29, 38
Mount Casino, 110
Mukhaliṅga, 40
Mūlamadhyamaka kārika, 72, 73, 85
Mysore, 36
Nāgahvaya, 67
Nāgalōka, 54, 70
Nāgānika, 39
Nāgārāja, 66
Nāgārjuna, 7, 8, 31, 46, 66, 67, 68, 69, 70, 71, 72, 74 75, 76 78, 79, 106, 107, 111, 113
Nāgārjunakoṇḍa, 36, 38, 42, 47, 50 51, 53, 55, 103, 104, 110, 115
Nāgās, 29, 32, 34, 54, 102
Naiyayika (logic), 88, 110
Nakamura, 83
Nalanda, 55, 89
Nānāghat, 39
Nandivarman, 114
Narayana, 114
Nārāyanaviṣṇu, 27
Nāsik, 41
Navavatāra panel, 115
Nellore, 86
Nikāya, 10, 12, 28, 29, 43
Nikāyabhēda vibhaṅga Vyākhyāna, 84
Nikāyasaṅgraha, 54
Nirmāṇakāya, 12
Nirvāṇā, 13, 16, 17, 28, 45, 46
Niṣāda, 40
Niyama, 27
Nyāya, 87
Nyayabindu, 91

Nyāyamukha (dvāra), 87
Nyāyāvārtika, 90
Orissa, 31, 32, 33, 55, 87
Paithan, 35
Paṅcamatikadhāra, 42, 43
Paramabhagavata, 114
Paramartha, 88
Paramartha satya, 76, 80
Pāramitā, 10, 13, 14, 18, 49, 55
Paratmasamata, 17, 18
Parivrajaka, 100
Pārkham, 30
Parthasāradhi misra, 88
Pātaliputra, 30
Paticcasamuppāda, 9
Paudanyapura, 65
Persian, 26
Ping-ki-lo (vengi)
Polytheism, 26
Poussin, 84
Prabhākari, 15
Pradīpa uddyotana nāmatīka, 84
Prajñā, 14, 17, 50
Prajñāpāramitā, 6, 7, 31, 32, 33, 54, 55, 70, 72, 73, 88, 108, 113
Prajñāpāramitāpiṅdārtha, 88
Prajñāpāramitā Saṁgraha, 88
Prajñāpradīpa, 8, 84, 85
Pramāṇa, 87
Pramāṇavārtika, 91
Pramāṇasamuccaya, 87, 90, 91
Pramudita, 15 16
Pranidāna, 14
Prapatti, 51
Prāsaṅgika, 66, 82, 83, 84
Pratiṣṭam 51, 52
Pratītyasamutapādahṛdaya, 72
Pratyeka Buddha, 13
Pubbasela,43
Pudgalaśūnyata, 7, 18, 31
Purushapura, 26
Pūrvaśaila, 43, 45, 46, 55
Puspagiri, 103
Rāga, 28
Rahulsamkrityayana, 89
Rājataraṅgiṇi, 69
Ratnakūta, 54
Ratnamēgha sūtra, 16
Ratnasaṁbhava, 12
Ratnāvali, 7, 72, 74, 106, 107
Roman, 37
Rudra, 40
Rūpakāya, 12
Sabbakāmi, 14
Saḍabhijña, 55, One who has achived six perfections
Saddharma, 8
Saddharmapuṇḍarīka, 6, 9, 11, 13, 54
Sādhumati, 15

Śaila schools, 55
Śailas, 43
Śaivism, 40, 41
Sakyamuni, 10
Salankayanas, 114
Sālihuṇḍam, 6
Samādhirāja, 6
Sāmantabhadra Bōdhicaryāvatāra, 54
Saṁbhōgakāya, 12
saṁbodhi, 1, 13, 15
Saṁgha, 4, 41, 42, 46
Samkhya, 80, 81, 85
Saṁkhyākārika, 88
Samudānika, 105
Samudiya, 103
Samvṛti satya, 76, 80
Samyuttanikāya, 2
Sanghadasi, 100
Sanghala, 100
Saṅgharakshita, 55, 82, 83
Śaṅkarācarya, 108
Śankaradigvijaya, 90
Sankaraswāmin, 87
Sanron sect, 82
Sarvajnānamārga, 7
Sarvamsūnyam, 19, 31
Sarvāstivāda, 30, 31
Sata śāstra, 80, 82
Sātānikōta, 35
Śātavāhanas, 3, 39, 40, 66, 100
Satya, 27
Sautrantikas, 32
Scythians, 3
Second saṁgiti, 4
Sekoddesatīka, 114
Selasaghasa, 43
Setagiri, 70
Siddhaṁ, 47
Siddhārthanika, 100
Sikṣāsamuccaya, 16
Śīla, 14, 27, 81
Sīlabhadra, 89
Simhala, 77
Simhavaktra, 86
Sir Charles Eliot, 3, 5, 10, 13, 39
Sing chao, 79
Śiva, 30, 40
Śiva Bhāgavatas, 40
Soul, 26
Śraddha, 29
Srāvakayāna, 5, 7
Sreṣṭhi, 3
Śrīkākuḷaṁ, 78
Śrīparvata, 43, 70, 106, 110, 115, 117
Śrīyajña Śātakarṇi, 69, 70
Sron brsan sgam po, 90
Stcherbatsky, 88, 89
Sthanakuṇḍur, 40
Sthaviravādin, 4
Stūpa, 15, 16
Sudarśana, 39
Sudurjaya, 15, 88
Suhṛllekha, 72, 74, 106
Sukhāvati, 71

Sukhāvativyūha, 6, 11
Sumanamāla, 66
Suṅgas, 3, 25, 40
Śūnyata, 1, 7, 8, 31, 46, 73, 74, 75, 76, 84, 108, 116
Sūnyatasaptati, 72
Sūrasena, 25
Surastra, 66, 110
Sūrya, 115
Sūtrakāra, 35
Suttanipāta, 33, 36
Suvarṇa prabhāsa, 6
Suzuki, 13, 14
Svabhāva, 31
Svātaṅtrika, 65, 82, 84, 85, 116
Swastika, 51
Tāmrapa, 105
Taṅtrāvārtika, 102
Tāntrika, 32
Tārā, 114
Tārānatha, 31, 32, 33, 89, 90, 109
Tarkajvāla, 84, 85
Tathāgata, 13, 28, 76, 88, 90
Tattvasaṅgraha, 32
Tena-Ka-che-ka, 109
Theravāda, 11, 116
Theravādins, 5, 31
Thērīgatha, 29
Thomas E. J., 26
Tibet, 13, 90
Tibetan tradition, 86, 87, 89
Tirumala Tirupati, 89
Trayatrimsa heaven, 104
Trikālapariksa, 87
Trikāya, 11, 12, 50
Triratna, 51
Tucci, 88
Tummalagudem, 113
Udyotakara, 88, 90
Udyotanasūri, 110
Upajjaya, 102
Upanishads, 28
Upapāduka, 12
Upāsaka, 17, 18, 100
Upāsika, 18, 103
Upāya, 14
Upāya kausalya, 14, 18
Uppuguṇḍur, 105
Vanijas, 105
Vāda, 87
Vaḍḍamānu, 38
Vaidalyasūtra and Prakaraṇa, 72
Vaipulya Sūtras, 6, 45, 116
Vairōcana, 12
Vaiśākhapūrnima, 113
Vaiśāradya, 49
Vaisesika, 79, 80, 81, 85
Vaiṣṇavism, 40, 41
Vaitulyavādins, 46
Vajjian monks, 4
Vajrapāni, 15
Vajrayāna, 114, 117

Vanijas, 105
Varuṇa, 26
Vasubandhu, 8, 9, 86, 87, 90, 92, 116
Vāsudeva cult, 25
Vāsudeva kṛṣṇa, 27, 28, 39
Vasumitra, 43
Vātsiputriya sect, 87
Vātsyayana, 88
Vēdali, 67
Vedaṅta, 85
Vedic, 25, 29, 39, 40
Vedula, 67
Vengi, 86, 87
Vetulyaka, 45, 46
Vidarbha, 66, 67
Vidyabhūsan, 90
Vigrahavyāvartani, 72, 73, 109
Vihāra, 51
Vijaya Śātakarṇi, 70
Vijaya Puri, 101, 105, 110
Vijñānavāda, 85, 88, 89, 116
Vikramasiṁhapura, 86
Vimala, 15
Vimalakīrti, 13, 14, 18
Vimalakīrtinirdēsa Sūtra, 13, 18
Vimānavatthu, 33
Vinaya, 4, 5, 43, 44
Vinītadēva, 43
Vipulartha Kankṣin, 104
Vīrāpuram, 35
Viśākha, 30
Visālamālavati, 87
Viṣṇu, 39, 40
Viṣṇuka, 39
Viṣṇukuṇḍin, 39
Viṣṇupālita, 39
Vrata, 40
Vyakta upadēsa, 2
Wisdom, 8, 15
Worship, 15, 16
Yaksas, 29, 34, 37, 38,
Yerraguḍi, 34
Yoga, 80
Yogācāra, 65, 89
Yogācāra bhūmiśāstra, 86
Yuan-chuang, 72, 77, 78, 83, 84, 85, 86, 89